Institute for Business Intelligence

Modelling and Reporting with SAP Business Information Warehouse 3.5

> Detailed introduction
> Practical functions
> Comprehensive, step by step case study

Lehmann, Peter; Freyburger, Klaus; Seufert, Andreas; Zirn, Wolfgang; Grasse, Sven; Suhl, Christian
Modelling and Reporting with SAP BW
Stuttgart, Steinbeis Edition 2006
ISBN 3-938062-44-4
ISBN 978-3-938062-44-9

Steinbeis Edition
Steinbeis Verlag
Willi-Bleicher-Str. 19
70191 Stuttgart
Germany

www.steinbeis-edition.de

Publisher:
Institute for Business Intelligence (IBI) - www.i-bi.de/EN
SAP (Switzerland) AG - www.sap.ch

Grafics: giraffo gmbh agentur für konzeption & kommuninkation
Print: Books on Demand GmbH

First printing, August 2006

Before You Start

SAP BW System Used

We used version SAP BW 3.5 IDES with Support Package 013.
The front end was SAP GUI 6.40 for Microsoft Windows with patch level 011
SAP BW was accessed using SAP BW BEx Analyzer 3.5 with patch level.

Support and Help

We created a link to a Web site for this case study on our Web site, www.i-bi.de.
The linked site contains additional, up-to-date information regarding case study
execution, as well as the data in csv file format. The links on the Web site are
intended primarily for instructors at colleges and universities who wish to use the
case study for teaching purposes. It also contains documents to help you prepare the
case study, as well as a document describing the authorization profiles – which we
would like to draw your attention in particular, as users of an SAP BW system at an
SAP University Competence Center. Because several institutions share the same
system, namespaces are needed to delimit the work areas. The authorization profiles
provide an additional layer of security.

We regret that First Level support is unavailable due to time constraints. But we
would be happy to receive any suggested corrections or advice by e-mail. Our
e-mail addresses can be found at our Web site at www.i-bi.de

Online help for the SAP BW system is available at http://help.sap.com

CONTENTS

Foreword

The SAP Business Information Warehouse, (SAP BW), has a leading position in software for the management of information systems. Going beyond the function as just the platform for the collection of basic business data, SAP BW becomes more and more important in the infrastructure of analytical applications. On the one hand, this book focuses on the procedure of modelling a system and in the other, on the functions for analysis and reporting of data.

We want to convey the basics about multidimensional information systems to the reader as well as to provide an overview of the functionality of SAP BW. This book neither claims to be a scientific textbook nor includes all the details of a complex software solution. Nevertheless, we are convinced that the reader will gain a deep understanding about the applications and the basic functions of an OLAP-system by studying this book. For that reason, this book focuses on the administration workbench as a modelling tool, on the potential of data analysis and on the reporting functions with the SAP BW Business Explorer Suite.

Accordingly, we chose to approach this topic, in a way, which differs from other publications on SAP BW. Step by step, we gradually introduce the functions of the software including a comprehensive case study for sales analysis. In our opinion, this approach allows for the transfer theory to the practical application model of the system. This book is addressed to everybody who wants to read up quickly, comprehensively and practically on SAP BW and therefore especially to decision makers and consultants as well as project collaborators and last but not least to lecturers and university students.

Our grateful thanks go to Mr. Sören Laub and Mr. Michael Fuhrmann, without whom, the creation of this book would not have been possible.

Stuttgart, Ludwigshafen, Zurich in Oktober 2006

I

Introduction To Enterprise Reporting

How to give an introduction to enterprise reporting? Let us start with a typical example.

It is ten in the morning, and you have to make a decision that will have a major impact on your product and sales strategies in the coming months. You know that the necessary information is available somewhere in the many information systems that you can access through your PC. But you also know that there is absolutely no chance that you will be able to collect and relate this information in the time available. Despite all your company's investments in hardware, software, networks and operating systems, you just can't get the information that you need to make informed decisions.

The reason for this is that most enterprise information systems are designed to meet the needs of the operational processes, such as sales and distribution, material management or accounting. The primary goal is to guarantee the smooth flow of day-to-day business data **into** the operational systems.

To achieve your goals, however, you need information from a variety **out of** operational data sources, in order to get a grip on the big picture.

We will use this example to introduce the business-related and technological basis for the subject of **business intelligence**. We will then implement an operational solution scenario based on a data warehouse, using SAP Business Information Warehouse as our primary application.

I

Fundamentals

We will first examine the current situation at the company and the importance of decision support systems, as well as their potential uses and critical success factors.

Status Quo

What is the situation at the companies like today? We will examine the situation from the aspects of competition, constantly changing markets, and changes to user groups.

Competitive Advantages

Information technology plays a key role in the search for new **competitive advantages**, as it no longer merely serves to collect and exchange data, but is also increasingly utilized for the rapid, systematic collection, management, dissemination, and interpretation of information. It can become a competitive factor in all phases of strategic decision-making processes if the company succeeds in suitably managing its critical success factors. To detect internal and external changes promptly, and possibly even predict them, decision-makers from all enterprise areas must have all relevant data and information available at the right time.

In addition to the competitive situation, the previous sellers' market is **turning into a buyers' market**, increasing the customers' impact on production. Customers expect high-value products, combined with improvements in ordering, warehousing, transportation, shipping, and acceptance service. It must be possible to analyze the business-relevant and process-relevant dimensions of these services. Because it is not possible to develop complete, predefined IT solutions for these new service-oriented activities, new demands for a new type of information technology are created.

These changes are leading to requirements for **"information on demand"** and **"ready to use"**, to close gaps in information supply at short notice and effectively exploit the potential of the information technology. In particular, in new organizational structures with flattened hierarchies in which decision-making competency is shifted "downwards", employees at all levels must be empowered to extract, transform (summarize, link, prepare) and analyze (compare and valuate) information from a wide range of sources independently.

The following user groups can currently be classified in accordance with their responsibilities:

- **Executives**: Require information for strategic decisions, such as the relation between market and supply. They need standard reports and exception reports with statistics, key figures, and so on immediately and flexibly, to execute their coordination and control tasks.

- **Decision-preparers**: This user group encompasses all activities involved in preparing decisions. For example, market researchers use data analysis to investigate existing and new fields of business, while business analysts reveal veiled correlations in data and use it to derive recommendations for executives.

- **Skilled employees**: Their areas of responsibility include activities in the planning and control of (partial) business processes at a company. In general, these are any activities that require a high level of specialist qualifications and competency.

- **Administrator**: They process detailed information regarding business objects in operative, day-to-day business, their development over time, business processes, and their costs and resources.

- **Support staff**: Their areas of responsibility include subordinate tasks to support regular operations.

Efficient, Effective Information Supply

To ensure **efficient, effective information supply**, existing IT landscapes have to be enhanced with an independent support system for the planning and decision-making level. Many companies implement a **data warehouse** as the main component of such expansions.

Note

The term **data warehouse** describes a database that is separate from the operative IT systems that serves as the enterprise-wide data basis for the entire spectrum of decision-supporting information systems.

Potential Benefits

The implementation of a data warehouse represents a significant investment for a company, consisting of the procurement costs for the required hardware and software and costs for in-house staff and external consulting support, and with a project length of several months to several years.

The decision to implement a data warehouse is often made according to strictly strategic aspects, as the following potential benefits of the data warehouse concept can help a company achieve its strategic goals.

Better Decisions

Better decisions due to more efficient information supply: The data warehouse provides the cornerstone from which employees at all levels – executive board, management, and specialist staff – can quickly and easily access the information they need to make their decisions. A data warehouse improves information supply for decision-makers qualitatively, quantitatively, and temporally (see next diagram).

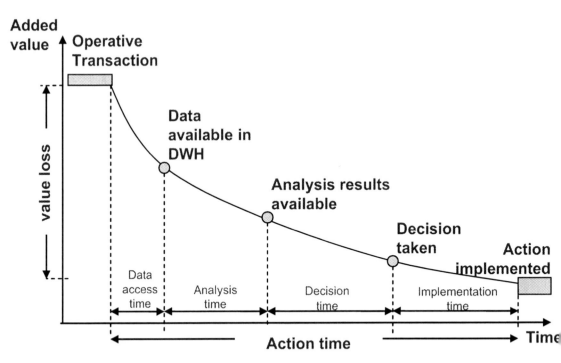

Figure: Potentials of Efficient Information Supply

The action time is defined as the period between entry of a business process (transaction) and a resulting measure. The action time consists of four time delays:

- **The data latency** describes the period that elapses until the data is available filtered, harmonized, and aggregated in the data warehouse.

- **The analysis time** is the interval required to provide the data to end users in the analysis systems.

- The end user can now retrieve this information and make decisions as necessary. The **decision latency** is often one of the longest delays.

- Based on the decisions made, specific measures can now be taken. The time elapsed until these measures are implemented is called the **implementation latency.**

Competitiveness

Increasing competitiveness: Because data is stored in a data warehouse over long periods, trends and their causes can be detected early on. This makes it possible to prevent negative developments and promote positive trends, for example, by using key figures as an early warning system to display deviations from predefined thresholds. End-user tools that interactively guide to the targeted information help reveal potential for productivity increases, cost savings, and optimization of business processes. Examples include periodic analyses or time series analyses, which can result in a consolidation of the market position or an increase in competitiveness.

Customer Satisfaction

Improvement of customer service and customer satisfaction: One example of using a data warehouse to improve customer service and customer satisfaction is the establishment of call centers, a method used primarily by companies in the service and retail sectors today. The focus is on the fast, flexible, reliable fulfillment of customer requests; the employee is in direct contact with the customer and assumes the function of an advisor. Data warehouse systems contain all the sales order data from the different operative systems, for example, store this data over a long period, and facilitate direct communication with the customer.

Collaboration

Improvement of collaboration at a company: In the past, the relationship between user departments, executives, and software specialists was frequently burdened by different perspectives and mutual mistrust. These obstacles have to be overcome in a data warehouse project.

Integrated Data Basis

Integrated data basis for decision-support systems: Using data from both enterprise-wide and external sources enables decision-makers to recognize and analyze complex, cross-area and enterprise-wide correlations, without having to worry about ensuring the consistency and quality of the examined data [Inmon (1994)]. The separation of decision support and operative data and systems means that analytics applications and their processing-intensive queries no longer access the datasets in the operative application systems, but instead use the data warehouse. This reduces the complexity of the operative applications, by splitting off the decision-support applications.

Fast Reporting

Fast queries and reports due to the data basis integrated in the data warehouse: The pre-aggregated data in the data basis of the data warehouse not only enables ad hoc reporting, but also results in faster response times in analytics applications. The repeated calculation of key figures is prevented, for example, thanks to the various aggregation levels available in the data bases. The requested information can be displayed directly on the end user's screen, without performance-intensive formatting, grouping, or sort routines.

Critical Success Factors

The success of a data warehouse implementation is determined by a series of critical success factors.

The sensible utilization of data is contingent on a number of **quality criteria**:

- **Precision**: The data must have a level of precision that is appropriate for the decision-makers area of activity. For example, all amounts in Financial Accounting have to be managed with two decimal places, while values are rounded to larger units in Sales Planning.

- **Completeness**: The decision-maker must be provided with the complete data. This is the only way to prevent wrong decisions due to missing data.

- **Context**: Data that has been extracted from its original environment and can no longer be related to it represents uncertain information for the decision-maker.

- **Accessibility**: Data is only useful to a decision-maker if it can be accessed quickly. Accessibility not only involves the technical and organizational prerequisites, but also options for filtering specific data from a data pool.

- **Flexibility**: It must be possible to compile, manipulate, and transform the stored data. It is not enough, for example, to provide the sales figures from a previous period broken down by production. Decision-makers must be enabled to break down these figures by further criteria according their individual needs, such as product group, sales channel, or user-defined periods.

- **Time and period relation**: Data must be provided to decision-makers in a timely manner, as delayed availability can reduce the benefit of information for a particular activity, or even render it useless. When history data is collected over a longer period, a much wider range of trend analyses is possible than with the short-term data taken from the operative systems. By detecting trends early, companies become able to react quickly to changes in their business environment, achieving a major competitive advantage over their rivals.

- **Transportability**: Data that is tied to a specific location or system is much less useful to decision-makers than data that can be transported and is thus available anywhere.

- **Security**: Data can give a company a competitive advantage over its rivals. Accordingly, it must be protected against unauthorized access.

When a company begins dealing with the activities involved in implementing a data warehouse, it often discovers that the exact definitions of business terms are not unique or unambiguous; specifically, the definition of a given term often varies from user department to user department. The term "open orders", for example, can quickly be misinterpreted between the sales and production areas if no other information is provided.

It is important to pay attention to the terminology in detail, to examine it, clarify its use in the individual application areas, and define uniform rules. Statements will be fuzzy, incorrect or contradictory if the terms they employ are fuzzy, incorrect or contradictory. In general, the following deficient terms can occur:

1. **Synonyms** are different expressions for the same concept. Customer and client, for example, both describe the same relationship to a business partner.

2. **Homonyms** are words that are spoke the same, but have much different meanings. Homonyms have to be dealt with and made distinguishable at the indicator level. Example: open orders from the sales perspective (open sales orders) and open orders from a production perspective (open production orders).

3. **Equipollencies** are terms that describe a concept from different perspectives, such as "vendor" and "supplier", and that usually have identical structures. Supplier is the term within procurement, while vendor is used in accounting. To ensure that no difficulties arise here, commonly used terminology must be developed.

4. **Ambiguities** arise when there is no clear separation between terms. Uncertainties occur with regard to the objects to which the terms apply. A specification of the content will result in better separation of the scope. Example: Do unconfirmed sales orders count as open sales orders?

5. **False designations**: The contents (meaning) of a term can change over time. If this change drifts widely from the "suggested" meaning of the original term, then comprehension difficulties will arise between users. Here one must make the effort and replace the familiar, yet no longer adequate meanings of a term with better ones.

Insufficient data quality is a frequent cause of wrong decisions. Even if the importance of quality is understood in theory, the sheer number of components in the data warehouse makes manual quality control practically impossible. In addition, different participants in a process have different quality preferences. The administrator of a data source is concerned with the high availability of a system, while a decision-maker wants to have the most up-to-date data possible.

Modern PC software has easy-to-use graphical user interfaces. Illustrated examples, used to demonstrate the tools at marketing events and seminars, reinforce this impression of simplicity. In particular, the accumulation of sales data in the context of time periods, regions, product groups and products is a particularly impressive demonstration when these figures are not only available in tables, but can also be displayed in histograms, pie charts, and so on at a click of the mouse. A frequently-observed side-effect: After such demonstrations, the user departments euphorically buy software tools, install them at the company, and are then confronted by the shocking reality. In fact, in reality it is a long road from demonstration example to specific use in a particular enterprise context. **"Buy and go" is a sure road to chaos.**

Other significant risks also lie outside of the software systems, such as:

- **Lack of interest** and motivation among executives and skilled employees

- **Lack of qualification** among the individuals who develop the system (system developers, software engineers), maintain it (system administrators), and ultimately use it (executives and skilled employees)

- **Lack of acceptance** and trust among users

- **Unsuitable organizational structure** (responsibility-oriented and process-oriented organization) within the company and/or at the executive/skilled employee level

- **Unsuitable task organization** and problem-solving structure in the application area

- **Lack of suitable models** and methods for modeling and dealing with problems

- **Lack of traceability of system use**, particularly deficient options for interpreting the gained results

- **Incorrect expectations** of the hardware and software technologies

- **Unsuitable technological infrastructure**, such as insufficiently powerful hardware and/or network structures

II

Some Terminology

This section introduces the important terms "business intelligence", "data warehouse" and "OLAP".

Business Intelligence

The term **Business Intelligence** has evolved in past years from mere fashion trend to a market that is increasing in importance. It describes a process intended to give better insight into a company and into functional chains.

Definition

> **Business intelligence** describes the integration of strategies, processes and technologies to generate success-critical information regarding status, potentials and perspectives from distributed, heterogeneous enterprise, market and competitor data.

Accordingly, the core of business intelligence is a process for enabling the near-time supply of relevant information to operational decision-makers for analytics and decision support. The basic idea is to feed the analysis results back into the operative and/or planning systems. The additional information gained supplements the datasets, making possible the effective support of other decision-makers as well.

If this process runs repeatedly, a knowledge base upon which enterprise decision and forecasts can be based is built, and changes constantly, not only boosting profits, but also the company's competitive position. The diagram below describes how the business intelligence process adds value to a company's data.

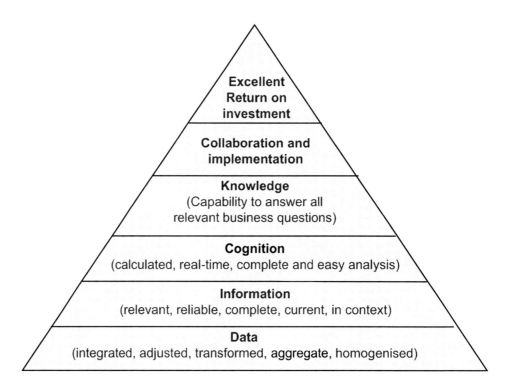

Figure: How Added Value Is Generated from Data

As the business intelligence pyramid shows, an appropriate solution has to be able to answer all the relevant business questions for the company to achieve a return on its investment. These business-related questions have to be specific to the company in question and reflect its specific business needs. Accordingly, the ability to model an enterprise structure as precisely as possible is a decisive factor for the success or failure of a data warehouse project.

Based on this process-focused view, we can identify three major technical process phases in which data is transformed to knowledge.

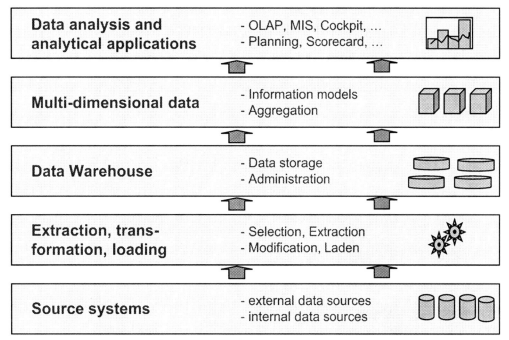

Data analysis and analytical applications	- OLAP, MIS, Cockpit, ... - Planning, Scorecard, ...
Multi-dimensional data	- Information models - Aggregation
Data Warehouse	- Data storage - Administration
Extraction, trans-formation, loading	- Selection, Extraction - Modification, Laden
Source systems	- external data sources - internal data sources

Figure: Technical Process Phases

Data Integration

The **data integration framework** deals with the extraction of data from upstream systems, its transformation, and its loading into a database (data warehouse).

The extraction step deals with connecting the data sources and transferring the data to a temporary store (staging area), where the subsequent (data) transformation steps can be carried out.

The transformation process changes the data that was extracted from the upstream systems, to support decision-making both on a logical/content-related and physical/technical basis. After the extraction and transformation steps run, the data is loaded into the data warehouse database – usually periodically . Depending on the application, the period can be monthly, daily, or even immediately after the data is generated in the upstream operative systems (i.e. in realtime).

Data Storage

The decision-relevant data is stored in a dedicated database – the data warehouse. The main idea here is to create a single, homogenous dataset to support decision-making by management. An important characteristic of the data warehouse is its **integration of distributed, heterogeneous information**, both internal and external. This not only involves the physical centralization of the data in a single data pool, but also its business context. While operative information systems are usually focused on business functions (such as materials management, sales and financial accounting), a data warehouse is structured according to issues and objects (products, customers, markets, and so on). Function-specific or department-specific views of the data warehouse are also called "data marts".

Data Utilization

The structure of a data warehouse and the preparation of the data serve one sole purpose: to portray decision-relevant information and process it further. The emphasis lies on the **users' varied requirements**.

To make relevant business information out of the data collected in the data warehouse, it has to be prepared accordingly. Several different levels of complexity have to be covered, with regard to both the tasks at hand and the relevant user groups: The spectrum ranges from the display of predefined reports for occasional users and rapid changes of the data perspective by experienced users to the support for complex data mining procedures for analytics experts.

What Is a Data Warehouse?

To ensure efficient, effective information supply, existing IT landscapes have to be enhanced with an independent support system for the planning and decision-making level. Many companies implement a **data warehouse concept** as the main component of such expansions.

Historical Development

The term "**data warehouse**" was first used in the early 1980s, in the context of "data supermarket" and "super databases". In 1988, IBM introduced an internal project it called the "European Business Information System", which it renamed in 1991 to "Information Warehouse Strategy". Its core represents the data warehouse concept. In the early 1990s, various hardware vendors – along with software and consulting firms – took up the data warehouse concept and offered it as a service package on a rapidly expanding market; concurrent debates regarding online analytical processing (OLAP) and the publications of Bill Inmon certainly also played a role.

Definition of Data Warehouse

What is a Data Warehouse?

A **data warehouse** is a secondary database that is generated from one or more operative databases with the aid of suitable extraction mechanisms. The data in this secondary database is prepared and aggregated to best meet the expected analyses.

The demand for analysis options requires an adequate modeling approach. This demand is frequently achieved through a multidimensional approach, to reflect the dimensions and hierarchies of the users' thinking. The data model of a data warehouse is expected to satisfy requirements for specialist focus, integration, non-volatility, periodicity, and redundancy.

Subject Orientation

Subject orientation: The choice as to which enterprise data will be collected in the data warehouse is based exclusively on management's information requirements, and not on functional areas or business processes developed for the individual application systems.

Integration

Integration: A fundamental problem in creating a data warehouse is the integration of the decision-relevant data from the various operative application systems to form a coherent collection of data. The application systems, which have grown and evolved over time, often contain radically different designations to describe the same concept (or identical designations for different concepts), as well as different coding, variable assignment, data attributes, key formats, and so on. Therefore, a data warehouse concept achieves consistent data storage (in the sense of standardized structures and formats) through various provisions during the data transfer.

Why standardize the structure?

Unique designations have to exist for all data in the data warehouse. A given data field in the data warehouse can have different, possibly inconsistent data sources in the operative systems, because the fields with identical data have different names in the different systems (synonyms) or different data fields have the same designations (homonyms).

Why standardize the format?

In addition to harmonizing up the data field designations, the different data formats have to be adjusted – for example, because:

- Certain attributes were defined with differing abbreviations during application development, for example, one application uses "m" for male and "f" for female, while another uses "0" and "1".

- Identical attributes in the individual operative applications are processed and saved with different value units for determining size and quantities, but the value unit is not documented and saved separately. Accordingly, a basic unit of measurement has to be defined for each attribute in the data warehouse, into which all the transferred size and quantity information can be transformed.

Non-Volatility

Non-volatility: Volatility describes the degree to which data changes during the course of regular usage. It measures either the average number of changes per time unit or the absolute number of changes in specific intervals. In contrast to conventional datasets, which are usually manipulated record by record, the data warehouse is fed with large amounts of current data from the operative systems at regular intervals. The data update itself usually takes place in the operative system. No data is maintained in the data warehouse itself, aside from certain data that is located only in the data warehouse (such as aggregated planning data). The non-volatile character of the data means that any evaluation and analysis can be traced and reproduced at any time.

Time Variance

Time variance: Whereas current data is only retained in operative datasets for short periods of time, the data warehouse records enterprise data over longer periods – for example, to enable comparative analyses of enterprise activity over a period of five or ten years. In contrast to operative datasets, suitable time characteristics are needed to describe the data. These characteristics can indicate specific points in time or intervals. In addition, end users can freely define the period for an analysis or evaluation.

Redundancy

Redundancy: In relational databases, relations are usually implemented in the third normal form to guarantee referential integrity and data consistency. The term "denormalization" describes a procedure in which the transition to the next normal form is reversed (or not performed at all) for practical reasons. The goal of denormalization is to reduce the number of database accesses required during an evaluation or analysis, thus reducing the load on the hardware and software and improving the overall response times of the data warehouse. The price for the performance gains are an increase in storage requirements for the denormalized data – caused by the creation of redundancies – and increased efforts for maintaining the referential integrity and data consistency.

Multi-Dimensionality

Without a semantic reference, the mere numbers of a key figure are meaningless. For example, the key figure "Sales Volume: USD 782,390" could involve last year's sales for one store or the total global sales of an entire division. The numbers only become comprehensible and useful to users when they are combined with other (objective) criteria (or characteristics) such as time, store, or division.

The logical arrangement of business key figures to form one or more objective criteria is called **multidimensionality.**

The criteria used to analyze a key figure are also called **analysis characteristics**.

A specific statement (query) involving a key figure that encompasses one or more objective criteria is called a **fact**.

We give some examples to illustrate the concepts introduced above.

- A multidimensional statement: "The sales volume in the motorcycle division in Switzerland amounted to exactly EUR 782,390 in December 2004."

- A key figure: **Sales volume in Euros**

- An analysis characteristics: **division, month and country**

The possibility of analyzing key figures from multiple perspectives, in near time and problem-oriented, contributes to optimized decision-making at a company.

What is OLAP?

What does the abbrevation "OLAP" mean?

OLAP is an acronym for **Online Analytical Processing**.

OLAP describes a software technology that gives managers and qualified employees from user departments fast, interactive, versatile access to relevant, consistent information.

Because OLAP systems have recently established themselves as the foundation for analytics applications in general and for planning software in particular, this section briefly describes the underlying methodology.

We will first explain pivoting, using a simple example.

Pivoting

A pivot table is an interactive table that can combine and compare large data volumes quickly. Columns and rows can be rotated to display different groupings of the source data, and the details of particularly relevant areas can be displayed.

Tables possess rows and columns, and are therefore said to be two-dimensional. The different rows contain the individual records, while the different columns contain their attributes. In the diagram below, gross and net sales of the stores are listed by country, month, division, and article.

	A	B	C	D	E	F	G
1	Example for Pivoting						
2							
3	CalYear/Month	Country	City	Subsidiary	Division	Product	Sales Quantity in Piece
4	JAN 2004	Switzerland	Zürich	Am Hardturm	Clothes	Protective clothing	148
5	JAN 2004	Switzerland	Zürich	Am Hardturm	Clothes	Helmets	87
6	JAN 2004	Switzerland	Zürich	Am Hardturm	Service	Technics	42
7	JAN 2004	Switzerland	Zürich	Glattzentrum	Motorbikes	Street cruise	17
8	JAN 2004	Switzerland	Zürich	Glattzentrum	Motorbikes	Moto cross	2
9	JAN 2004	Switzerland	Zürich	Glattzentrum	Motorbikes	Vespa	25
10	JAN 2004	Germany	Magdeburg	Südring	Clothes	Leather jackets	532
11	JAN 2004	Germany	Magdeburg	Südring	Clothes	Helmets	342
12	JAN 2004	Germany	Magdeburg	Südring	Service	Technics	213
13	JAN 2004	Germany	Frankfurt	Kaisersstrasse	Motorbikes	Street cruise	231
14	JAN 2004	Germany	Frankfurt	Kaisersstrasse	Motorbikes	Moto cross	421
15	JAN 2004	Germany	Frankfurt	Kaisersstrasse	Motorbikes	Vespa	123
16	FEB 2004	Switzerland	Zürich	Am Hardturm	Clothes	Leather jackets	132
17	FEB 2004	Switzerland	Zürich	Am Hardturm	Clothes	Helmets	96
18	FEB 2004	Switzerland	Zürich	Am Hardturm	Service	Technics	83
19	FEB 2004	Switzerland	Zürich	Glattzentrum	Motorbikes	Street cruise	48
20	FEB 2004	Switzerland	Zürich	Glattzentrum	Motorbikes	Moto cross	32
21	FEB 2004	Switzerland	Zürich	Glattzentrum	Motorbikes	Vespa	38
22	FEB 2004	Germany	Magdeburg	Südring	Clothes	Leather jackets	653
23	FEB 2004	Germany	Magdeburg	Südring	Clothes	Helmets	432
24	FEB 2004	Germany	Magdeburg	Südring	Service	Technics	327
25	FEB 2004	Germany	Frankfurt	Kaisersstrasse	Motorbikes	Street cruise	321
26	FEB 2004	Germany	Frankfurt	Kaisersstrasse	Motorbikes	Moto cross	431
27	FEB 2004	Germany	Frankfurt	Kaisersstrasse	Motorbikes	Vespa	452

Figure: Table with Rows and Columns

Relevant questions that this data could answer include: Which articles are selling well, or in which countries is a particular product selling poorly?

They are easy to answer, by simply totaling the records for the respective countries. This results in the following table:

	A	B	C	D	E
1	Sales by country and product in 2004				
2					
3	Product	Switzerland	Germany	Italy	France
4	Protective Clothing	1.776	6.384	5.107	7.022
5	Helmets	1.044	4.104	3.283	4.514
6	Technics	504	2.556	2.045	2.812
7	Street cruise	204	2.772	2.218	3.049
8	Moto cross	24	5.052	4.042	5.557
9	Vespa	300	1.476	1.181	1.624

Figure: Sales by Country in 2004

What about sales per article and country, broken down by month? We supplement the data view with analysis characteristic "month", and can then view article sales ordered by month. When we imagine the individual monthly views arranged one after another, the next step is to examine the cells of the various tables as parts of a cube.

Sales by country in 2004

March 2004

Product	Switzerland	Germany	Italy	France
leather jackets	432	893	2.312	1.023
helmets	234	1.023	832	2.341

February 2004 ... ...

Product	Switzerland	Germany	Italy	France
leather jackets	134	653	104	432
helmets	96	432	601	963

January 2004 ... ...

Product	Switzerland	Germany	Italy	France
leather jackets	148	532	123	535
helmets	87	342	531	1.241
technics	42	213	1.242	421
street cruise	17	231	64	134
moto cross	2	421	16	1.422
vespa	25	123	1.439	12

Figure: Sales by Month

Cube Metaphor

The views shown above involve three two-dimensional tables. This results in a cube, similar to the one shown below.

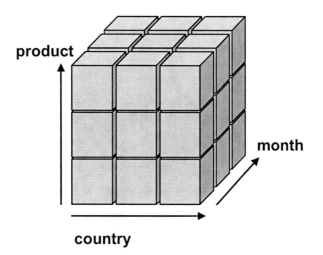

Figure: Cube with Dimensions Product, Country and Month

This cube has three dimensions, designated here as **product**, **country** and **month**. When we lay the tables above onto the cube's coordinate system, the columns are arranged along the x-axis. The articles are distributed along the y-axis. The months are distributed among the z-axis, to emphasize the fact that the tables are arranged one after another. Therefore, the axes of the cube encompass a three-dimensional space, in which an intersection of the individual coordinates assumes the facts of a specific "cell".

Accordingly, this "cube" is nothing more than three reports, generated from table data and arranged to resemble a cube. So far, the table contains much more information than the cube. Of course, we could generate additional dimensions from the remaining data, but what good is it to know that there is a store on South Street if you don't know which city it is in? Moreover, a cube consisting of the dimensions country, city and store would be fairly empty, because the value combinations of country, city and store would surely only fill a few cells of the coordinate space. It is therefore sensible to use these table columns to form a new, common dimension – such as "sales region".

We could proceed similarly with the "month" dimension: it would also be helpful, for example, to display the data as summarized quarterly and annual values.

We assign the articles to a division and group them in a dimension called "product".

We would then have a true OLAP cube with the three dimensions product, sales region and time. The difference to the above cube is that in addition to their different names, the dimensions now also have additional levels. Specifically, there are other cells in the cube, which can be calculated from the previous ones. As such, the "sales region" dimension contains three additional levels: country, city and store. The "date" dimension also has three levels: year, quarter and month. Finally, the "product" dimension has two levels: division and article.

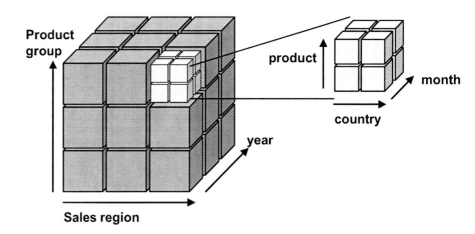

Figure: Cube with Dimensions Sales Region, Article, Time

Now that we have created the cube, we have to clarify what it will be used for. Firstly, we can create reports, which can be comprised from any combination of individual elements from the various dimensions.

	A	B	C	D	E
1	**Sales by division and country**				
2					
3	**Division**	**Switzerland**	**Germany**	**Italy**	**France**
4	+ clothes	1.748	6.548	3.652	4.479
5	+ Service	2.386	12.495	8.764	15.087
6	+ bikes	365	1.247	14.652	4.532
7	+ finance services	653	70.485	58.743	34.373
8	+ papers & books	43.653	2.485	5.743	3.373
9	+ ...	...	...	...	...
10					
11					

Figure: Sales by Division and Country

The above figure shows sales by division and country. The + symbol indicates the option of navigating to further levels. It would be good to know, for example, which articles of clothing are sold most frequently in each specific country. This question can be answered by clicking the + symbol.

Sales by division and country

Division	Switzerland	Germany	Italy	France
+ clothes	1.748	6.548	3.652	4.479
- leather jackets	474	2.213	1.203	1.835
- helmets	674	1.831	846	1.347
- gloves	273	1.832	833	846
- accessories	327	672	770	451
+ Service	2.386	12.495	8.764	15.087
+ bikes	365	1.247	14.652	4.532
+ finance services	653	70.485	58.743	34.373
+ papers & books	43.653	2.485	5.743	3.373
+ ...	...	...	...	...

Figure: Sales by Division, Article and Country

The report can be adjusted at the click of the mouse. This is called "navigation" within the report, as the report can be conceived as a sub-cube that still possesses the structures of the cube. We will now introduce the basic navigation functions.

The first option is rotation, or pivoting. As the diagram below shows, this means rotating the "cube" on an axis, making visible a different combination of two dimensions. A two-dimensional view of the data cube, which corresponds to displaying one face of the cube, is often sufficient for analyses. Whereas the combination of dimensions "product and sales region" is visible at first, the combination of dimensions "product and time" are shown after rotation.

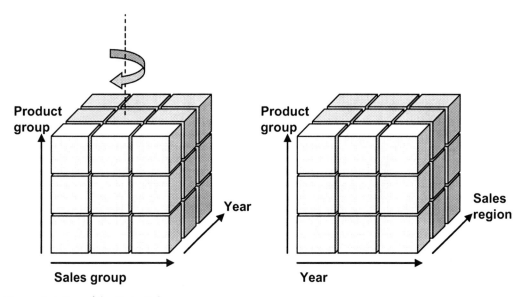

Figure: Rotation of the Data Cube

A **slice** is a set of data that is cut out of the data cube. Setting a **filter** for an element of a dimension creates a view of a clearly defined slice. As the figure below emphasizes, this can be a view of **all products** and all months that have the value "Switzerland" at the country level of the sales region dimension.

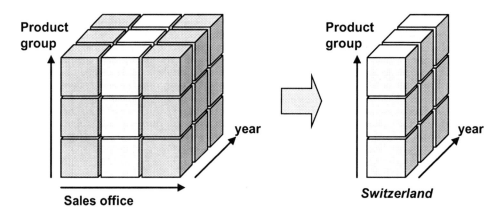

Figure: Slice of sales region dimension at country level with element "Switzerland"

Even though the right-hand portion of the figure above looks like a slice, it is also a data cube. The levels city and store also exist below Switzerland, while the product dimension has levels division and article, and the time dimension has the levels year, quarter and months.

Dice

A **dice** is a **multidimensional slice** of a cube. Several dimensions are restricted to one level each. Instead of a "slice", data dicing results in a **sub-cube**. One example is the creation of a multidimensional view of sales for a specific division in a specific country in a specific quarter (see diagram below). The selected dataspace can be used, for example, for a plan/actual comparison of the current year. It contains all **products** from the product group called **clothes**, all **subsidiaries** in the sales region **Switzerland** and all **quarters** in year **2004**.

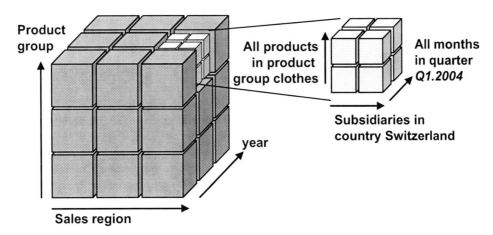

Figure: Dice in the dimensions product group (into level product with filter on product group = "clothes"), sales region (into level: subsidiaries with filter on sales region = "Switzerland") and time (into level quarters with filter on year = "2004")

Rollup and Drilldown

The levels of a dimension can often be summarized and grouped. Months are grouped together to form quarters (and, turn, quarters to years) and products to product groups. This creates a hierarchical ordering schema that can be used for the mathematical aggregation of key figure values. The rollup and drilldown operators are available to navigate in this type of hierarchy.

Drilldown means breaking a selected element down one level further, to display the underlying elements.

	Switzerland	Germany	Italy	France
1. Quarter	1.748	6.548	3.652	4.479

Drill-Down   **Roll-Up**

	Switzerland	Germany	Italy	France
January	348	1.438	953	1.238
February	532	2.434	1.234	1.543
March	868	2.676	1.465	1.698

Figure: Rollup and Drilldown Operators

The rollup function describes the opposite approach, navigating from one aggregation level to a higher level (from month to quarter to year, for example).

Criteria for OLAP

The term "OLAP" was originated by Edgar F. Codd in 1993; he initially defined it based on 12 rules. A few of the primary rules are described below.

Multi-Dimensionality

Analogous to the natural view of an analyst, an OLAP product must enable a **multi-dimensional perspective** – that is, an OLAP model should enable multi-dimensional structures. Reports also have to be fast and easy to change. The operations for navigating through multi-dimensional dataspaces play a major role.

Transparency

If an OLAP system accesses heterogeneous datasets – such as multiple data warehouse systems – this has to take place **transparently** (that is, unnoticed) for the end user. It must not matter whether the application is integrated or not. Likewise, the use of multiple data source must not have any negative impact on the functional scope, performance, or usability of the system.

Multi-User Capability

It must be possible for **several users to access a dataset** at the same time, while not endangering either data integrity or data security. This demands an authorization concept that can take a wide range of end-user profiles into account.

Cross-Dimensionality

All calculations should be possible over **multiple dimensions**, regardless of how many (or what type of) dimensions are involved. In particular, cross-dimensional calculations are often required to determine key figures and key figure systems.

Users must be given an **easy-to-use interface** and must be able to navigate through the dataset quickly and easily. The drilldown and rollup operators play a major role here.

Spreadsheet vs. OLAP

Many companies maintain that their spreadsheet programs, such as Microsoft Excel, do their job well, and therefore represent a cheap alternative to OLAP software. When we examine the requirements in more detail, however, the limits of the spreadsheet programs are quickly reached.

- Not suited to several (or many) concurrent users

- Poor performance when processing large volumes of data

- Poor performance during data aggregation: aggregation is always performed on the client PC

- No authorizations defined at the cell or value level

- No support for metadata to describe the additivity of key figures; for example, different quantities (kg, liters, and so on) and amounts (euros, USD, and so on) can usually be added "seamlessly"

- Difficult, complicated integration of multiple data sources

Operative Information Systems vs. OLAP

In the early 1980s, a dominant notion dictated an all-encompassing database system could lie at the center of all enterprise application systems. It was quickly determined that the demands of database systems for operative applications differ widely from those for decision-support systems.

The operative systems are the foundation for every business IT application. The working methods in these operative systems are focused on the processing of transactions, which means specific functional areas can be supplied with control data quickly and precisely. They are designed to achieve maximum processing efficiency of a company's relatively static day-to-day business, which is characterized by a large number of transactions and access to only a few data records.

Unsuitable Parameters	The underlying database systems for operational applications are configured technically to deal with a high transaction throughput, whereas decision-support systems have to read a large number of records. In turn, this requires specific configuration and parameterization that is often the opposite of those required for operative applications.

Unsuitable Scheme	Another relevant aspect is that the data schemas of the operative systems are focused on business process flows and functions. These data schemas are less suited to decision-makers, because they are designed to facilitate the fast, secure entry of transactional data. Effective, efficient support of the planning and decision-making level is therefore often difficult with existing data schemas, because their structures are easy to understand. The granularity of the data is too great, and the environment too heterogeneous, to quickly enable a recipient-oriented view of the company.

No Time Modeling	Furthermore, operative data is overwritten daily, which means an important dimension – time – is lost as a reference.

Unsuitable for Users	Finally, we have to consider that the way the preparation of the data is not easy for the end user to understand or use as an information source.

Overview	Some comparison of the differences between transaction-oriented and decision-oriented data is summarized in the table below.

Transaction-oriented systems	**Decision-oriented systems**
Application-oriented	Subject-oriented
Detailed data	Summarized, aggregated data
High precision at time of access	Variable values, snapshots (different time spots)
Used by operative staff	Used by decision takers
Data will be overwritten	Data will not be overwritten (version management)
Is used regularly and repeatedly	Is used irregularly
Processing methods are known beforehand	Processing methods are not known beforehand

Targeted access primarily of single records	Targeted access of multiple (many) records
Driven by transactions	Driven by analysis
Redundancy is undesired	Redundancy is necessary and is controlled by the application
Small data volumes used for each processing run	Large data volumes used for each processing run

Table: Differences Between Transaction-Oriented and Decision-Oriented Information Systems

III

Reporting Systems

Reporting systems are end-user tools that support the establishment of a reporting system.

Query Tools

Simple query tools, such as those in office applications, make it possible to create (generate) database queries quickly and with little effort. The logical database structure and language constructs of a query language are hidden from the end user, behind a graphical user interface. These tools often include basic slice and dice functions for online data analysis (OLAP). Due to the limited options available for formatting the query results, however, these tools are only suitable for setting up a reporting system if they are combined with other report generators.

Report Generators

Report generators are tools that feature options for supplementing content and appearance, beyond strict query functions. There are design options, such as adding headers and footers, placement of tables and images, and the flagging of particularly striking values (exception handling). They usually build on relational systems, which they offer support for formulating SQL queries. Graphic editors (such as "query by example" techniques) assist with the generation of correct SQL syntax. In general, these tools offer limited semantic support, and differ mainly in the scope of SQL commands they support.

MQE Tools

The further development of report generators resulted in the **managed query environment** (MQE) approach. MQE tools already offer more semantic support – meeting user demands for intuitive, easy-to-use tools – because the data is represented as information objects. A data abstraction layer lets you hide the physical database structures, enabling subject-specific display of the data based on enterprise terminology. End users do not to know anything about the underlying database structure, and can cover their information demands by freely combining information objects. Because the underlying logical data model is hidden, only SQL queries with correct syntax are generated, and semantic faults are even prevented, for example, because a join can only be specified if it corresponds to the data model. A reporting server is frequently a component of an MQE environment. It controls the periodic or aperiodic activation of reports, organizes and monitors the distribution of the reports (authorization concept), and documents the development history of the generated reports. Negative factor: The abstraction layer has to be set up and maintained manually. Moreover, these tools are also subject to restrictions in the scope of SQL commands. Complex multi-dimensional operations such as rotation or drilldown and rollup are only supported partially, if at all.

OLAP Tools

In contrast to MQW tools, which merely display data and have a relatively narrow range of analyses, **OLAP tools** feature intuitive, flexible, extremely powerful analytics functions. Users can examine the relevant data in a user-defined form, observe it, and thus monitor the company's critical factors. The multi-dimensional view of the data makes it possible to run versatile analyses over every dimension of the data. OLAP functions range from simple rotation and drilldown to complex enterprise analyses (time series analyses, regression, and so on), and the resulting data can be displayed in various graphics (pie chart, bar chart, surface diagram, vertical bar chart, and so on) and analyzed further. Thanks to their powerful functional scope and ability to organize and manage the large data volumes in a data warehouse efficiently, OLAP tools represent one of the most state-of-the-art front end solutions for data warehouses.

IV Technical Architecture

In most cases, the data server's structure corresponds to one of the following architectural types:

Central Data Warehouse

A **central data warehouse** is one physical data basis, which exists in parallel to the operative datasets. Whenever a data warehouse is mentioned, the implication is always one central data warehouse.

Data Mart

A **data mart** is a subject-specific or department-specific data warehouse. In contrast to a central DW, it does not store all of a company's data. Instead, the data is distributed to several small, local data warehouse servers that contain the data marts. The additional management effort required, such as the essential data synchronization, is offset by the advantage that the user departments have flexible access to their data, which is often very specific.

Virtual Data Warehouse

The concept of the **virtual data warehouse** involves direct access of the operative data systems by the end user – which actually contradicts the basic concept of reducing the load on the operative systems. There is no data warehouse in the sense of secondary data storage; hence the term "virtual". The benefit here is rapid, cost-effective realization, because the operative data does not have to be transformed and no new technical infrastructure has to be purchased. The major disadvantage is that the end users' queries are run on a database that is designed for rapid data entry. Therefore, complex queries over multiple tables will result in massive performance problems.

II

Semantic Modeling

This chapter deals with the semantic modeling of multi-dimensional systems. The primary question is how the requirements of an application area can be recorded and described (specified) to enable plans for building a data warehouse.

It first describes a general life-cycle model of a data warehouse, and identifies the design phases. A general introduction to the subject of data modeling follows. We will then turn our attentions to multi-dimensional data modeling. A case study will be used to describe how to proceed.

I

The Business Dimensional Lifecycle Model

Kimball's business dimensional lifecycle model [Kimball et al. (1998); Kimball/Ross (2002)] is often used to implement data warehouses.. The following diagram illustrates the main phases of the model:

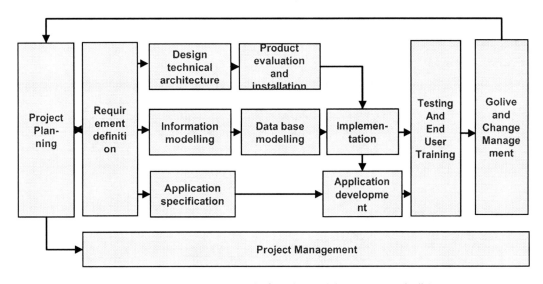

Figure: Business Dimensional Lifecycle Model (Source: Kimball/Ross (2002), p. 332)

Project Planning

The first phase of the life cycle is project planning. It involves preparing the company for the implementation of the DW by examining questions regarding the justification, dimensioning, and staffing of the project. In addition to project planning, ongoing, in-process project management is an essential component for ensuring the proper execution of the project, as well as detecting potential deviations from the schedule in a timely manner (Kimball/Ross (2002), p. 334-340).

Definition of Requirements

Understanding and fulfilling the end users' demands are essential to the success of the project. Therefore, the definition of requirements first involves defining the target group, and then using the proper methods to determine their requirements. The close interdependency between project planning and definition of requirements is indicated by the dual arrow between these two phases.

Technical Design

Technical design involves defining the requirements of the data warehouse's technical structure, by discussing questions such as data distribution, performance, data volumes, and so on. Based on this information, a suitable product that meets these requirements is selected in the second step. The selection may involve methods and instruments such as product valuation matrices, market analyses, and prototypes [Kimball/Ross (2002), pp. 347-353].

Logical Design

The logical design of the model deals with the question of how the data for storage will be structured and how it will get into the data warehouse. The first step is semantic and logical data modeling, applying multi-dimensional modeling concepts. The logical data models are implemented in the system during physical modeling. The ETL (extraction, transformation, load) design is responsible for ensuring that both master data and transaction data are sent seamlessly from the source systems to the data warehouse [Kimball/Ross (2002), pp. 353-362].

Application Design

The main task in the application design area is the specification and development of the end-user applications that will build on the data warehouse. These applications have to meet the users' requirements defined at the beginning of the project. In addition to ergonomics and usability, this phase also involves concepts such as Web access and information portals[Kimball/Ross (2002), pp. 362-364].

Distribution

The data warehouse is implemented through training activities and rendered support. This is decisive in the overall project success, because this phase determines whether or not the product is accepted [see Kimball/Ross 2002, p. 364f.].

Maintenance and Growth

Lastly, the model contains the problems posed by maintenance and growth of a data warehouse, which could result in a follow-up project that starts the whole cycle over again. It primarily involves the design of ongoing support for the data warehouse end users, along with release management and change management [see Kimball/Ross (2002), p. 365f.].

II

Data Modeling

While a variety of methods and procedures have been developed for operative systems to establish appropriate semantic data models that are as independent of the specific system environments as possible, data warehouse projects often neglect the fact that reliable documentation is a major factor determining both the ease of maintenance and ease of use of a system. It is all too easy to use graphics tools to build a "demonstration façade" that thrills the decision-makers and makes them want more, fast. But the time needed for a clear, conceptual data model is then missing. The widespread success of semantic models with multi-dimensional data structures make these deficits are all the more regrettable.

Why Data Modeling?

During the system setup, data models serve as a basis for discussions between user department staff and IT specialists. Moreover, the derived semantic, multi-dimensional data models can be used as navigation aids in the data warehouse. Due to their near independence from individual tools, these data models guarantee that the collected knowledge of the data structures will be retained and reused even if releases, tools or personnel change. Lastly, when it comes time to make modifications to the data structures, semantic models can offer valuable orientation assistance and simplify the changes.

What Is a Data Model?

But, what is a data model?

Data Model

A **data model** is described as "a structured map of the data from a strictly delimited part of perceived reality that is relevant for a specific application or users, including the relationships between them".

Levels of Data Modeling

Semantic data models are the result of a conceptual design, and generally represent natural-language statements that are independent of the technology of the data store or end-user tools selected later.

Unfortunately, when data warehouse systems are developed today, "the same mistakes are made today as when operative IT systems were designed 30 years ago: the data structures are designed for very specific applications and products".

Therefore, to ensure data independence, the subjective specification of a data warehouse should be completely disassociated from the technical knowledge required to implement it. Usually, the following project phases and modeling levels are named for the setup of an information system:

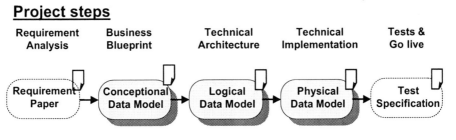

Figure: Project Phases and Modeling Levels to Set Up Information Systems

Semantic Data Model

The development of an information system begins with the user's terminology; a requirements analysis results in program specifications.

Clarification of the specialist terminology converts the requirements to a technical concept. At the end of this process, a semantic (conceptual) data model is constructed that models the relevant facts of the challenge at hand, but still independent of the database system. As such, the semantic data model also forms the interface to the system's users. Therefore, the decisions in this layer as to which key figures and which analysis criteria are relevant, and which correlations exist between them, have to be made from the user's perspective and in the user's language. The entity-relationship model (ERM) has proven to be an effective semantic modeling tool.

Logical Data Model

The technical system draft transforms the technical concept to the solution concepts for the IT implementation. At this level, the semantic data model is reformulated to satisfy the demands of a specific database system. This model is also called a "database schema". Due to the simple transition from ERM to relation model, these models are often used together. The logical data model is often specified in a chart language or pseudo-code to structure the future system.

Physical Data Model

Lastly, the technical implementation is the description of the specific hardware/software-specific realization of the logical data model at the physical level. It deals with aspects of physical storage, as well as memory/access optimization. Normally, this step is completed using a programming language (such as SQL Data Definition Language).

III

Multi-Dimensional Data Modeling

Based on the structuring of the data modeling levels, the **following procedure** can be identified for data warehouse design:

1. Analyze the required information
2. Develop the semantic data model
3. Develop the logical data model
4. Develop the physical data model

Structures of Multi-Dimensional Data

The literature differentiates between the following object categories that are required as descriptive elements for multi-dimensional data models:

*   **Business key figures** and their interlinkage
*   **Business dimensions**, dimension **attributes** and dimension structures (**hierarchies**)

- **Derivation rules** for the relevant, content-based transformation of data

Key Figures

The term key figure is used synonymously with a number of other terms, including variables, facts, measures and measured facts [Kimball (1996), p. 22], although each of these terms also has other meanings. In the following, the concept of key (business) performance indicators is meant.

Today, a variety of key figures assists decision-makers at every level and in all enterprise areas, by providing quantitative figures to help them carry out their activities. A key figure is a figure "with concentrated power to forecast, plan, monitor and control a system". Business measurements are not analyzed in isolation; they are tightly interwoven and related to one another in a variety of ways. The set of these correlations is called a key figure system or key figure schema, and displayed as a key figure tree. The diagram below shows an example with the Du-Pont key figure schema.

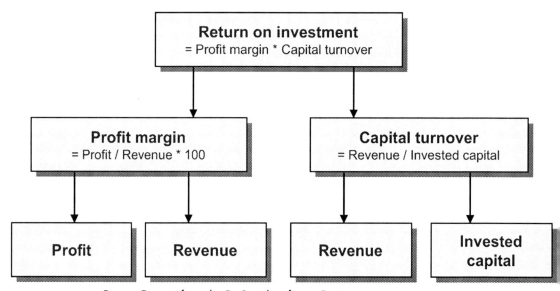

Figure: Excerpt from the Du-Pont key figure System

Key figures possess descriptive attributes (such as unit of measure or value range), calculation rules, format specifications, and an "exact" description. If this content information is defined carefully, this will create a comprehensive, consistent key figure structure to serve as the starting point for further analysis. It is essential that each key figure is supported by an unambiguous, unmistakable term definition. A typical example is the homonymous use of the term "open orders", which represents two completely different process key figures from the perspective of the sales department ("sales orders") and the production department ("production orders").

Analysis Characteristics

Without a semantic reference, the mere numbers of a key figure are meaningless. Only in connection with other (objective) criteria do the digits become comprehensible and useful to users. The logical structuring of key business figures to form one or more objective criteria, such as customer, article, region, or time period, is called multi-dimensionality. These criteria, which are related to key figures and used to analyze them, are also called analysis characteristics.

Attributes

Analysis characteristics are often described in more detail through properties (attributes). A store, for example, has a store manager, is located in a certain city, has an address with street and house number, and is assigned to a company code.

Note that data analysis with an attribute is not always sensible, because no useful information can be obtained without the semantic relation to other attributes. What good is it to know how high the sales of a store in a certain street are if you don't know the city? In contrast, it may make sense to analyze sales by store manager, for example, when it comes to calculating the pending salary increases.

Dimensions and Hierarchies

Analysis characteristics often have a hierarchy relationship to one another. The different levels of a hierarchy relationship are often called consolidation levels, because key figures are consolidated (aggregated) along a consolidation level through totaling or the calculation of averages.

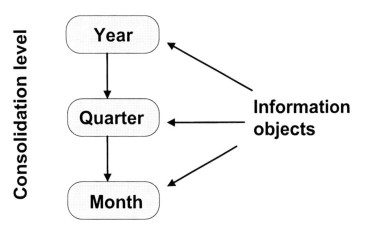

Figure: Hierarchy Relationship Between Analysis Criteria

43

We can now form a separate dimension from each analysis characteristic. But this results in the loss of structural information that is required for the data analysis functions (drilldown, slice & dice, and so on).

It therefore makes sense to take analysis characteristics that have hierarchy relationships and group them together in a dimension. These groupings form the dimension structure, creating the foundation for the navigation paths along the consolidation level in the dimension.

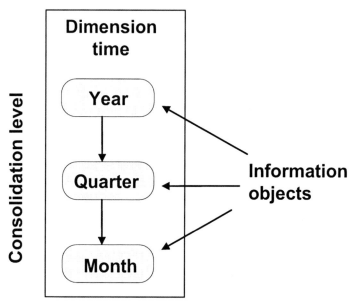

Figure: Dimension

Additivity of Key Figures

Key figures such as sales volume in euros or sales in units are characterized by the fact that they are added together during navigation along a consolidation path within a dimension. The sum of all sales in the months from January 2004 to December 2004 is the same as the sum of all sales in the four quarters of the year 2004. This key figure is therefore considered "additive".

The number of employees is an example of a non-additive key figure. The number of employees at the end of the 1st quarter 2004 is very different from the sum of the number of employees at the end of each month. The "number of employees" key figure is not additive with regard to the time dimension, but would be additive for a dimension that describes the sales organization, for example. The number of employees in the individual stores can be added together to calculate the number of employees in a country. This type of key figure is called "semi-additive".

Key figures that represent ratios, such as profit margins, are not additive in any dimension, and are therefore called "non-additive".

During hierarchy modeling, problems occur continually due to ignored modeling anomalies. Moreover, the deployed database system cannot deal with these special structures in many cases.

Unbalanced hierarchy trees can result in serious aggregation errors during drilldown and rollup that are not apparent at first glance. The sales department staff (vielleicht besser "Sales Person" verwenden, da diese Bezeichnung (SPe) auch im Screenshot unten benutzt wird) can be organized in sales groups, for example, while the introduction of sales groups may be deemed unnecessary in smaller sales organizations. When the sales revenues are aggregated to sales groups, the sales by salespersons not assigned to a group may not be identified.

A cyclical consolidation path is said to occur when the different shares of dimension elements result in a hierarchy that is no longer unambiguous after rollup. This is often the case in investment accounting, for example, in which the reciprocal deliveries are allocated by share. This problem has to be solved in the application software.

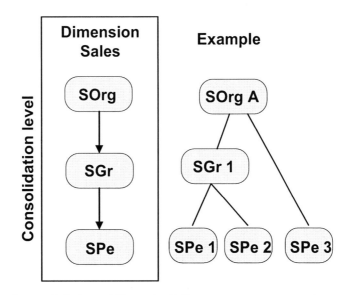

Figure: Unbalanced Hierarchy (Left)

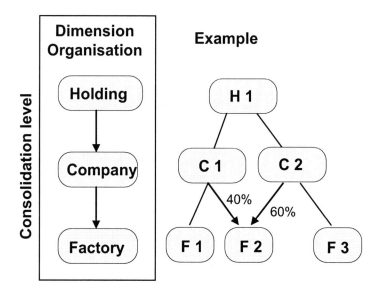

Figure: Cyclical Consolidation Paths (Right)

A further anomaly occurs when the elements in a level are not formulated free of overlaps. For example, different, non-disjunctive customer groups can be formed from the customer master records. As a result, revenues from a customer would be tracked in both customer groups during aggregation, leading to incorrect results in this parallel hierarchy.

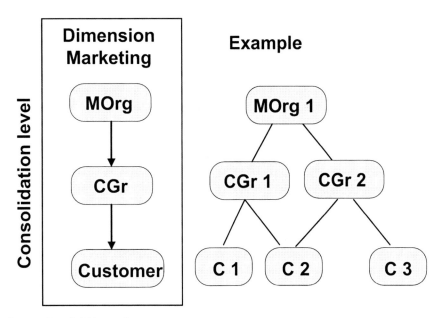

Figure: Parallel Hierarchy

Slowly Changing Dimensions

The modeling of multi-dimensional structures is frequently dependent on business requirements. The version management of master data plays an important role here. While the display of current attributes is the most frequently implemented requirement, objects change over time in real life. Therefore, the key date-specific display of attributes is part of the daily routine for a data warehouse.

This historical display of attributes is called slowly changing dimensions. You will learn about different requirements and modeling methods in this section.

Case Study

We are examining a scenario in which each salesperson works in a specific sales office. They can change offices over time.

Example

Mr. Huber worked at the Magdeburg sales office until February 28, 2005.
Mr. Huber began working at the Montreux sales office on March 1, 2005.
Mr. Schulze began working at the Magdeburg sales office on March 1, 2005.

Sales Person	Sales Office
Bauer	Magdeburg
Huber	Magdeburg
Maier	Montreux
Schmidt	Montreux

Sales Person	Sales Office
Bauer	Magdeburg
Huber	Montreux (verändert)
Maier	Montreux
Schmidt	Montreux
Schulze	Magdeburg (neu)

Assignment in 02.2005   **Assignment in 03.2005**   **today**

Figure: Changes of Salesperson Assignment to Sales Office Over Time

We now have to ask ourselves what happens to the sales figures when the sales person changes sales offices. Management has described the following requirements:

- Current view: "I only care about which sales office the salesperson belongs to when I execute the query." This means the sales that a salesperson made when working in a different sales office are also displayed in the query for the new sales office.

- Historical truth: "I care about which sales office the salesperson belonged to when he/she made the sale." This means the sales remain with the sales office that was valid at the time.

- Time dependency: "I want to be able to define a key date. The report should be based on the sales office at that time." As a result, we can estimate how the sales office's sales might have been if the salesperson had not changed offices.

Current View

A manager who wants the current view is only responsible for the situation at execution time. She does not care about historical development. This simplifies comparisons with past periods (such as the previous year). As such, her report is formed exclusively with structures from March 2005.

If every manager at a company only needs the current display, there is no real need for version management of the master data. As such, the master data can simply be overwritten.

We can analyze a salesperson's sales figures as an example. When Mr. Huber changes sales offices, all his sales are allocated to his current sales office, although he worked in another office previously. In the current display, the data assignments that are valid at the time of the query are always displayed.

Assignment in 02.2005

Sales Person	Sales Office
Bauer	Magdeburg
Huber	Magdeburg
Maier	Montreux
Schmidt	Montreux

Assignment in 03.2005

Sales Person	Sales Office
Bauer	Magdeburg
Huber	Montreux
Maier	Montreux
Schmidt	Montreux
Schulze	Magdeburg

Umsätze in 02.2005 und 03.2005

Sales Person	Month	Revenue
Bauer	02.2005	100.000
Huber	02.2005	150.000
Maier	02.2005	90.000
Schmidt	02.2005	100.000
Bauer	03.2005	140.000
Huber	03.2005	120.000
Maier	03.2005	100.000
Schmidt	03.2005	150.000
Schulze	03.2005	200.000

Current view

Sales Office	Sales Person	Month	Revenue
Magdeburg	Bauer	02.2005	100.000
		03.2005	140.000
	Schulze	03.2005	200.000
	Result		**440.000**
Montreux	Huber	02.2005	150.000
		03.2005	120.000
	Maier	02.2005	90.000
		03.2005	100.000
	Schmidt	02.2005	100.000
		03.2005	150.000
	Result		**710.000**

Figure: Example of the Current View

The above diagram shows the analysis. The selected data (03/2005) is used for the analysis. The previous assignments (02/2005) are not used.

Historical Truth

A manager who needs the historical truth is someone who needs the historical assignment within the period as well. The data is displayed as it is saved in the database.

Because Mr. Huber changed sales offices, he is listed twice in the query: once with his sales in the old office and once in the new office. In contrast to the key date-specific analysis, the individual records in the sales table are displayed with the valid values for the historical assignment in the historical truth view.

Version management of the master data is required in order to generate this query.

Assignment in 02.2005	
Sales Person	**Sales Office**
Bauer	Magdeburg
Huber	Magdeburg
Maier	Montreux
Schmidt	Montreux

Assignment in 03.2005	
Sales Person	**Sales Office**
Bauer	Magdeburg
Huber	Montreux
Maier	Montreux
Schmidt	Montreux
Schulze	Magdeburg

Revenues in 02.2005 und 03.2005		
Sales Person	**Month**	**Revenue**
Bauer	02.2005	100.000
Huber	02.2005	150.000
Maier	02.2005	90.000
Schmidt	02.2005	100.000
Bauer	03.2005	140.000
Huber	03.2005	120.000
Maier	03.2005	100.000
Schmidt	03.2005	150.000
Schulze	03.2005	200.000

Historical View

Sales Office	Sales Person	Month	Revenue
Magdeburg	Bauer	02.2005	100.000
		03.2005	140.000
	Huber	02.2005	150.000
	Schulze	03.2005	200.000
		Ergebnis	**590.000**
Montreux	Maier	02.2005	90.000
		03.2005	100.000
	Huber	03.2005	120.000
	Schmidt	02.2005	100.000
		03.2005	150.000
		Ergebnis	**560.000**

Figure: Example of the Historical Truth

In the historical truth view, the sales are allocated according to the assignment at the time of the transaction.

Key Date-Related View

A manager who needs a key date-related display cares about the situation on a specific key date (predefined dates or times can also be defined, such as quarter, end of month, year, and so on). This analysis is similar to the current display, with the difference that a past date is used instead of the current date.

This display makes it possible to reconstruct past queries, such as the query from February 28, 2005. The sales person still belonged to the Magdeburg office at that time. If the set of sales data to analyze is also restricted to February 28, 2005, we get the following result:

Assignment

Sales Person	Sales Office
Bauer	Magdeburg
Huber	Magdeburg
Maier	Montreux
Schmidt	Montreux

Assignment in 03.2005

Sales Person	Sales Office
Bauer	Magdeburg
Huber	Montreux
Maier	Montreux
Schmidt	Montreux
Schulze	Magdeburg

Revenues in 02.2005 und 03.2005

Sales Person	Month	Revenue
Bauer	02.2005	100.000
Huber	02.2005	150.000
Maier	02.2005	90.000
Schmidt	02.2005	100.000
Bauer	03.2005	140.000
Huber	03.2005	120.000
Maier	03.2005	100.000
Schmidt	03.2005	150.000
Schulze	03.2005	200.000

Key date-related assignment: 28.02.2005
Key date revenue: 28.02.2005

Sales Office	Sales Person	Month	Revenue
Magdeburg	Bauer	02.2005	100.000
	Huber	02.2005	150.000
		Result	250.000
Montreux	Maier	02.2005	90.000
	Schmidt	02.2005	100.000
		Result	190.000

Figure: Example of a Key Date-Related View

The effects of a change can also be traced. It might be useful, for example, to simulate the situation as if the salesperson hadn't changed offices. To do so, we specify a key date that stipulates the salesperson's assignment to the Magdeburg sales office (such as February 28, 2005), but do not restrict the sales data; the result shows the revenues from the sales office as if the assignment from 02/2005 were still current. We can therefore simulate what a report would look like if the sales person hadn't changed. To compare, we then select the current view.

Assignment in 02.2005

Sales Person	Sales Office
Bauer	Magdeburg
Huber	Magdeburg
Maier	Montreux
Schmidt	Montreux

Revenue in 02.2005 und 03.2005

Sales Person	Month	Revenue
Bauer	02.2005	100.000
Huber	02.2005	150.000
Maier	02.2005	90.000
Schmidt	02.2005	100.000
Bauer	03.2005	140.000
Huber	03.2005	120.000
Maier	03.2005	100.000
Schmidt	03.2005	150.000
Schulze	03.2005	200.000

Assignment in 03.2005

Sales Person	Sales Office
Bauer	Magdeburg
Huber	Montreux
Maier	Montreux
Schmidt	Montreux
Schulze	Magdeburg

Key date-related assignment: 28.02.2005
Key date revenue: today

Sales Office	Sales Person	Month	Revenue
Magdeburg	Bauer	02.2005	100.000
		03.2005	140.000
	Huber	02.2005	150.000
		03.2005	120.000
	Schulze	03.2005	200.000
		Result	**710.000**
Montreux	Maier	02.2005	90.000
		03.2005	100.000
	Schmidt	02.2005	100.000
		03.2005	150.000
		Result	**440.000**

Figure: Example of a Key Date-Related View

Technical Implementation

The following technical options are available to implement this reporting requirement:

- Adapt the historical data material to the new structures. The old structures are lost in the process.

- Save the historical dataset. Old analyses can be retrieved, but at the price of a larger data volume and a more complex update.

- Set up parallel hierarchies. This enables old values to be displayed with any structures.

- Version management with time stamp. Enables maximum flexibility in reporting. A disadvantage is the drop in performance caused by analyzing the data variations over time.

We will return to the subject of implementation again in a later chapter.

Methodological Approach

Although transaction-based modeling using an entity relationship model (ERM) appears to differ widely from the modeling in a multi-dimensional data model, entity relationship models are an elegant way to create a multi-dimensional data model for later implementation in the data warehouse.

The reason for the often overwhelming complexity of ERMs is that a single display often models several business processes at the same time. In many cases, for example, order receipt, goods issue, invoice issue, and payment receipt are displayed in a single ERM, although these processes can never take place at the same time. We therefore use a methodology to create (construct) an ERM that merely has to model one view of the relevant control factors of a business process. The results of the requirements analysis are then shown [Kimball et al. (1998), p. 146]. The following procedure is used:

Step 1: Situation assessment

Step 2: Define terminology

Step 3: Form dimensions

Step 4: Display as multi-dimensional dataspace

We will use our case study to describe the procedure.

Modeling the Case Study

We will now reiterate the basics of multi-dimensional modeling, based on our case study.

Motorsport AG is a mid-sized company with its head office in Magdeburg. The company produces motorcycles, and also deals in accessories. It has two subsidiaries, in Munich (Motorsport München GmbH) and Montreux (Motorsport Montreux S.A).

The company sells its products to retailers and distributors. In addition, the company recently opened another sales channel for direct sales in the Internet. The motorcycles and accessories from the head office in Magdeburg are sold at the sales offices "Bike Studio Magdeburg" and "Bike Studio Berlin". Sales of the Munich subsidiary are handled through the "Motorcycles München" sales office. Sales in Montreux take place at the studio "de Velomoteur".

To achieve quantity discounts in procurement, the raw materials and parts for the in-house production of motorcycles are procured centrally. In contrast, the accessories are procured locally, to react faster and more flexibly to the customers' different needs on site.

The diagram below shows a typical monthly report, which the head of the Sales department receives from the IT department via e-mail. It basically looks like all the other reports he receives. If he wants detailed information, he has to retrieve it laboriously and directly from the sales processing system.

Sales data for month 01.2005

Month	Company Code	Country	Sales Office	Distribution Channel	Division	Product	Sales Person	Revenue	Revenue net	Discount	Quantity	Price
01.2005	Motorsport GmbH	Germany	München	Wholesale	Clothes	Jacket XL 2341	Mr. Huber	9.519,94 EUR	8.567,94 EUR	952,00 EUR	21 PC	226,67 EUR
01.2005	Motorsport GmbH	Germany	München	Wholesale	Helmets	Helmet KS 199	Mr. Huber	8.856,50 EUR	7.970,85 EUR	885,65 EUR	22 PC	205,96 EUR
01.2005	Motorsport GmbH	Germany	München	Wholesale	Technics	TÜV	Mr. Huber	10.050,89 EUR	9.045,81 EUR	1.005,08 EUR	16 PC	257,71 EUR
01.2005	Motorsport GmbH	Germany	München	Wholesale	Street cruise	XKR 2000	Mr. Huber	278.509,19 EUR	250.658,27 EUR	27.850,92 EUR	29 PC	19.207,53 EUR
01.2005	Motorsport GmbH	Germany	München	Wholesale	Moto cross	VS 1388	Mr. Huber	310.510,36 EUR	279.459,33 EUR	31.051,03 EUR	38 PC	16.342,66 EUR
01.2005	Motorsport GmbH	Germany	München	Wholesale	Vespa	RS 1000	Mr. Huber	121.672,53 EUR	109.505,27 EUR	12.167,26 EUR	42 PC	5.793,94 EUR
01.2005	Motorsport GmbH	Germany	München	Retail	Clothes	Jacket XL 2341	Mr. Huber	7.479,94 EUR	7.105,94 EUR	374,00 EUR	16 PC	249,33 EUR
01.2005	Motorsport GmbH	Germany	München	Retail	Helmets	Helmet KS 199	Mr. Huber	6.796,85 EUR	6.457,00 EUR	339,85 EUR	18 PC	226,56 EUR
01.2005	Motorsport GmbH	Germany	München	Retail	Technics	TÜV	Mr. Huber	9.071,57 EUR	8.617,99 EUR	453,58 EUR	14 PC	283,49 EUR
01.2005	Motorsport GmbH	Germany	München	Retail	Street cruise	XKR 2000	Mr. Huber	285.231,82 EUR	270.970,23 EUR	14.261,59 EUR	27 PC	21.128,28 EUR
01.2005	Motorsport GmbH	Germany	München	Retail	Moto cross	VS 1388	Mr. Huber	323.584,47 EUR	307.405,25 EUR	16.179,22 EUR	36 PC	17.976,92 EUR
01.2005	Motorsport GmbH	Germany	München	Retail	Vespa	RS 1000	Mr. Huber	137.026,44 EUR	130.175,12 EUR	6.851,32 EUR	43 PC	6.373,32 EUR
01.2005	Motorsport GmbH	Germany	München	Internet	Clothes	Jacket XL 2341	Mr. Huber	9.370,33 EUR	8.714,40 EUR	655,93 EUR	22 PC	240,26 EUR
01.2005	Motorsport GmbH	Germany	München	Internet	Helmets	Helmet KS 199	Mr. Huber	7.641,30 EUR	7.106,41 EUR	534,89 EUR	18 PC	218,32 EUR
01.2005	Motorsport GmbH	Germany	München	Internet	Technics	TÜV	Mr. Huber	12.566,10 EUR	11.686,55 EUR	879,63 EUR	24 PC	273,18 EUR
01.2005	Motorsport GmbH	Germany	München	Internet	Street cruise	XKR 2000	Mr. Huber	366.479,67 EUR	340.826,09 EUR	25.653,58 EUR	36 PC	20.359,98 EUR
01.2005	Motorsport GmbH	Germany	München	Internet	Moto cross	VS 1388	Mr. Huber	251.186,53 EUR	233.603,48 EUR	17.583,05 EUR	29 PC	17.323,20 EUR
01.2005	Motorsport GmbH	Germany	München	Internet	Vespa	RS 1000	Mr. Huber	135.114,44 EUR	125.656,42 EUR	9.458,02 EUR	44 PC	6.141,56 EUR
01.2005	Motorsport Schweiz AG	Switzerland	Montreux	Wholesale	Clothes	Jacket XL 2341	Mrs. Hemmi	11.277,72 CHF	10.149,95 CHF	1.127,77 CHF	18 PC	375,92 CHF
01.2005	Motorsport Schweiz AG	Switzerland	Montreux	Wholesale	Helmets	Helmet KS 199	Mrs. Hemmi	6.831,86 CHF	6.148,68 CHF	683,18 CHF	10 PC	341,59 CHF
01.2005	Motorsport Schweiz AG	Switzerland	Montreux	Wholesale	Technics	TÜV	Mrs. Hemmi	15.387,14 CHF	13.848,43 CHF	1.538,71 CHF	19 PC	427,42 CHF
01.2005	Motorsport Schweiz AG	Switzerland	Montreux	Wholesale	Street cruise	XKR 2000	Mrs. Hemmi	366.340,42 CHF	329.706,38 CHF	36.634,04 CHF	23 PC	31.855,68 CHF
01.2005	Motorsport Schweiz AG	Switzerland	Montreux	Wholesale	Moto cross	VS 1388	Mrs. Hemmi	338.803,57 CHF	304.923,21 CHF	33.880,36 CHF	25 PC	27.104,28 CHF
01.2005	Motorsport Schweiz AG	Switzerland	Montreux	Wholesale	Vespa	RS 1000	Mrs. Hemmi	91.287,71 CHF	82.158,94 CHF	9.128,77 CHF	19 PC	9.609,24 CHF
01.2005	Motorsport Schweiz AG	Switzerland	Montreux	Retail	Clothes	Jacket XL 2341	Mrs. Hemmi	14.059,55 CHF	13.356,58 CHF	702,97 CHF	18 PC	413,52 CHF
01.2005	Motorsport Schweiz AG	Switzerland	Montreux	Retail	Helmets	Helmet KS 199	Mrs. Hemmi	10.896,81 CHF	10.351,97 CHF	544,84 CHF	18 PC	375,75 CHF
01.2005	Motorsport Schweiz AG	Switzerland	Montreux	Retail	Technics	TÜV	Mrs. Hemmi	11.754,06 CHF	11.166,36 CHF	587,70 CHF	14 PC	470,16 CHF
01.2005	Motorsport Schweiz AG	Switzerland	Montreux	Retail	Street cruise	XKR 2000	Mrs. Hemmi	578.180,75 CHF	549.271,71 CHF	28.909,04 CHF	33 PC	35.041,26 CHF
01.2005	Motorsport Schweiz AG	Switzerland	Montreux	Retail	Moto cross	VS 1388	Mrs. Hemmi	402.498,63 CHF	382.373,70 CHF	20.124,93 CHF	27 PC	29.814,72 CHF
01.2005	Motorsport Schweiz AG	Switzerland	Montreux	Retail	Vespa	RS 1000	Mrs. Hemmi	163.837,42 CHF	155.645,55 CHF	8.191,87 CHF	31 PC	10.570,16 CHF
01.2005	Motorsport Schweiz AG	Switzerland	Montreux	Internet	Clothes	Jacket XL 2341	Mrs. Hemmi	11.157,42 CHF	10.376,40 CHF	781,02 CHF	14 PC	398,48 CHF
01.2005	Motorsport Schweiz AG	Switzerland	Montreux	Internet	Helmets	Helmet KS 199	Mrs. Hemmi	11.586,83 CHF	10.775,75 CHF	811,08 CHF	14 PC	362,09 CHF
01.2005	Motorsport Schweiz AG	Switzerland	Montreux	Internet	Technics	TÜV	Mrs. Hemmi	14.498,10 CHF	13.483,24 CHF	1.014,86 CHF	14 PC	453,07 CHF
01.2005	Motorsport Schweiz AG	Switzerland	Montreux	Internet	Street cruise	XKR 2000	Mrs. Hemmi	422.087,87 CHF	392.541,72 CHF	29.546,15 CHF	25 PC	33.767,02 CHF
01.2005	Motorsport Schweiz AG	Switzerland	Montreux	Internet	Moto cross	VS 1388	Mrs. Hemmi	359.131,77 CHF	333.992,54 CHF	25.139,23 CHF	25 PC	28.730,54 CHF
01.2005	Motorsport Schweiz AG	Switzerland	Montreux	Internet	Vespa	RS 1000	Mrs. Hemmi	193.529,96 CHF	179.982,86 CHF	13.547,10 CHF	38 PC	10.185,78 CHF

Figure: Sales Manager's Monthly Report

The head of the Sales department is dissatisfied with the existing IT solution. In particular, he criticizes:

- Poor availability for staff working in the field

- Poor performance of the existing reports

- Varying, unclear definitions of the different key figures

- Insufficient report flexibility with regard to filtering and grouping criteria

- Insufficient timeliness (monthly report instead of daily report)

- Complex handling of different currencies (EUR, CHF)

- Lack of historical sales trends

He needs several days at the start of every month to analyze the reports he receives and draw up his monthly report to management.

Initial Situation Analysis

Step 1

An analysis of the current reports in which the key figures and analysis criteria are recorded results in the following picture. The key figures and characteristics in bold type were taken from the above monthly report for the sales manager.

Reports

	Sales Planning	Monthly Sales Rep	Production Report	...		Remarks
Key Figures						
Revenue	X	X				Which currency? How calculated?
Revenue net	X	X				Which currency? How calculated?
Price	X	X				Which currency? How calculated?
Discount	X	X				Which currency?
Sales Quantity	X		X			Which unit?
Internal Product Price			X			Which currency? How calculated?

	Sales Planning	Monthly Sales Rep	Production Report	...		Remarks
Information Objects						
UOM	X		X			Unit of product
Produkt No			X			Product No in sales
Product description	X					Product description in sales
Division	X					Division the product belongs to
Year		X	X			4-digit year description
Quarter		X	X			Quarter the month belongs to
Month	X	X				Month in format JJJJ.MM
Sales Organisation	X					Grouping of distribution channels
Sales Store	X					Description of sales office
Store Manager	X		X			Manager of sales office
Country	X					Country of sales office
Region	X					Company code for sales office
Currency	X					Currency of company code

Define terms

Figure: Situation Assessment of Reporting Requirements

Definition of Terminology

Step 2

When data from different sources is grouped together in consolidated form, it is essential that the terms used be clear and agreed upon. According to a study by "The Conference Board", a business association, and Price Waterhouse, an enterprise consulting firm, more than half of all data warehouse projects fall behind schedule or get bogged down completely. The most difficult step is to cleanse the production data and prepare it such that all users can understand it. As a result, the establishment of a data warehouse provokes discussions about terminology, promoting a common understanding of the business.

Language defects such as synonyms (must be recorded), homonyms (must be eliminated), equipollencies (must be discovered), ambiguities (must be rendered more precisely) and incorrect designations (must be replaced) must be detected and dealt with. The difficult is in harmonizing company terminology with the new definitions. While enforcement of the new terminology standards is usually difficult, it is the only to ensure overall acceptance of the new application system. A uniform understanding of the underlying terms is even more significant in the information analytics system, because the described information objects represent the direct, unmistakable interpretation of the key figure (systems).

Key figures	Definition
Revenue	The revenue is the sum of revenues after
Revenue net	Revenue net = Revenue - Discounts. Excluding
Price	Product price = revenue / sales quantity. The
Discount	In general, discounts are given to customers whic
Sales Quantity	The sales quantity is given in base unit of measur
Internal Product Price	The internal product price serves the internal

Information Objects	Definition
UOM	Unit of product. The unit is determined at finished
Produkt No	Product No in sales. It has 8 digits and is
Product description	Product description in sales. The materials logistic
Division	Division the product belongs to. The classification
Year	4-digit year description
Quarter	Quarter the month belongs to. Format: Q.JJJJ
Month	Month in format JJJJ.MM
Sales Organisation	Grouping of distribution channels
Sales Store	Description of sales office
Store Manager	Manager of sales office. Time-dependent classific
Country	Country of sales office
Region	Company code for sales office. Classification for
Currency	Currency of company code. The conversion categ

Figure: Definition of Terminology

Forming Dimensions

It is now time to create the structures to organize the set of analysis characteristics. The OLAP cube can then be generated from the structure. To keep our example from becoming unnecessarily complicated, we will limit the number of analysis characteristics to the set of characteristics in the above sales view. In reality, the information requirements analysis can easily result in a list with 80 or more analysis characteristics.

Step 3

It first makes sense to roughly group the analysis characteristics and use them to create common dimensions. Article, base unit of measure and division are terms that will have something to do with a product. Year, quarter and month are time-related terms. Distribution channel, sales office, etc. are terms that come from sales. We group the key figures together under the sales analysis heading.

Of course, we could also have assigned the division to the sales dimension, or called the product dimension article instead. We also could have structured the key figures differently: We could have grouped the price information together under the price analysis heading.

The primary factor here is the cooperation with the end users who will ultimately use the OLAP cube.

Sales Analysis	Key Figures
	Revenue
	Revenue net
	Price
	Discount
	Sales Quantity
	Internal Product Price

	Information Objects
Product	Product
	Product description
	Division
	Unit of Measurement
Time	Year
	Quarter
	Month
Sales	Distribution Channel
	Store
	Sales Manager
	Country
	Region
	Currency

Figure: Forming Dimensions

Multi-Dimensional Dataspaces

The key business figures are numerical values that form the centerpiece of the data analysis. They generally represent monetary values or quantities that occur over time, through business transactions. In contrast, dimensions have a descriptive nature. They enable different views of the key figures and make it possible to group and analyze them differently. Dimensions possess analysis characteristics that frequently have hierarchy relationships with one another.

The diagram below shows a format that is used frequently in entity relationship modeling.

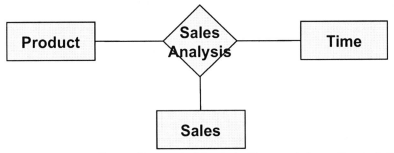

Figure: Portrayal of Analysis Characteristics as Simple Entity Relationship Model

At the semantic level, the dimensions represent the entity types, while the OLAP cube represents a complex relationship type of the involved entity types.

III

Logical Modeling

In general, the data warehouse can be any database system that is suited to processing extremely large volumes of data. In practice, this generally involves relational or multi-dimensional databases that have been extended specifically to process warehouse data. This chapter introduces these two types of database systems in order to emphasize the requirements of such systems for data warehouses.

I

Relational OLAP (ROLAP)

Relational OLAP means that the data is stored in tables that are related to one another through keys – as usual in relational database management systems (DBMS). In the process, the multi-dimensional data is mapped to database structures (or database schemes) in a special way, called a star schema.

Star Schema

The star schema is an approach for storing multi-dimensional database structures in relational database systems [Kimball (1996), p. 10ff].

The underlying concept of the star schema is the classification of data into two groups: facts and dimensions. Facts are generally numeric and are the focus of the data analysis. Dimensions, in contrast, have descriptive character, and represent the relevant analysis characteristics.

Both data groups – facts and dimensions – are stored in tables. The center of the star schema is the fact table and its corresponding data, which represents the key figures to analyze. A table for each dimension is arranged around the fact table and linked only with that fact table. This creates a star-shaped arrangement of the tables. As a result – in an analogy to the multi-dimensional cube – the fact table contains the same values as the cells of the cube. The number of possible records in the fact table corresponds to the number of occupied cells.

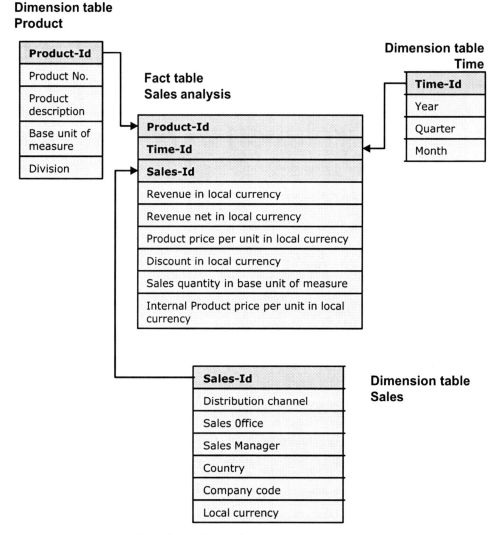

**Dimension table
Product**

Figure: Example of a Star Schema

The above diagram shows the star schema from our case study. The fact table
has a primary key that is composed from the involved dimension tables. Each
dimension table has one or more attributes, in addition to a primary key.

The following diagram shows the content of the dimension tables.

Dimension table PRODUCT

Product-Id	Product No	Product Descr	Division	Unit of Measurement
1	123953	Jacke XL 2341	Clothes	Piece
2	423432	Helm KS 199	Helmets	Piece
3	848329	TÜV	Technics	Piece
4	784750	XKR 2000	Street cruise	Piece
5	784500	VS 1388	Moto cross	Piece
6	785374	RS 1000	Vespa	Piece

Dimension table TIME

Time-Id	Month	Quarter	Year
1	01.2005	Q1	2005
2	02.2005	Q1	2005
3	03.2005	Q1	2005
4	04.2005	Q2	2005
5	05.2005	Q2	2005
6	06.2005	Q2	2005

Dimension table SALES

Sales-Id	Sales Channel	Store	Sales Manager	...
1	Wholesale	München	Mr. Huber	...
2	Retail	München	Mr. Huber	...
3	Internet	München	Mr. Huber	...
4	Wholesale	Montreux	Mrs. Hemmi	...
5	Retail	Montreux	Mrs. Hemmi	...
6	Internet	Montreux	Mrs. Hemmi	...

Fact table SALES-ANALYSIS

Product-ID	Time-ID	Sales-ID	Revenue	Revenue net	Discount	Qty	Price
1	1	1	9.519,94 EUR	8.567,94 EUR	952,00 EUR	21 PC	226,67 EUR
2	1	2	8.856,50 EUR	7.970,85 EUR	885,65 EUR	22 PC	205,96 EUR
3	1	3	10.050,89 EUR	9.045,81 EUR	1.005,08 EUR	16 PC	257,71 EUR
4	1	1	278.509,19 EUR	250.658,27 EUR	27.850,92 EUR	29 PC	19.207,53 EUR
5	1	2	310.590,36 EUR	279.459,33 EUR	31.050,03 EUR	38 PC	16.342,66 EUR
6	1	3	121.672,53 EUR	109.505,27 EUR	12.167,26 EUR	42 PC	5.793,94 EUR
1	1	1	7.479,94 EUR	7.105,94 EUR	374,00 EUR	16 PC	249,33 EUR
2	1	2	6.796,85 EUR	6.457,00 EUR	339,85 EUR	18 PC	226,56 EUR
3	1	3	9.071,57 EUR	8.617,98 EUR	453,58 EUR	14 PC	283,49 EUR
4	1	1	285.231,82 EUR	270.970,23 EUR	14.261,59 EUR	27 PC	21.520,28 EUR
5	1	2	323.584,47 EUR	307.405,25 EUR	16.179,22 EUR	36 PC	17.976,92 EUR
6	1	3	137.026,44 EUR	130.175,12 EUR	6.851,32 EUR	43 PC	6.373,32 EUR
1	1	1	9.370,33 EUR	8.714,40 EUR	655,93 EUR	22 PC	240,26 EUR
2	1	2	7.641,30 EUR	7.106,41 EUR	534,89 EUR	18 PC	218,32 EUR
3	1	3	12.568,38 EUR	11.688,55 EUR	879,83 EUR	24 PC	273,18 EUR
4	1	1	366.479,67 EUR	340.826,09 EUR	25.653,58 EUR	36 PC	20.359,98 EUR
5	1	2	251.186,53 EUR	233.603,48 EUR	17.583,05 EUR	29 PC	17.323,20 EUR
6	1	3	135.114,44 EUR	125.656,42 EUR	9.458,02 EUR	44 PC	6.145,56 EUR
1	1	4	11.277,72 CHF	10.149,95 CHF	1.127,77 CHF	18 PC	375,92 CHF
2	1	5	6.831,86 CHF	6.148,68 CHF	683,18 CHF	10 PC	341,59 CHF
3	1	6	15.387,14 CHF	13.846,43 CHF	1.539,71 CHF	19 PC	427,42 CHF
4	1	4	366.340,42 CHF	329.706,38 CHF	36.634,04 CHF	23 PC	31.855,68 CHF
5	1	5	338.802,57 CHF	304.923,21 CHF	33.880,36 CHF	25 PC	27.104,28 CHF
6	1	6	91.297,71 CHF	82.158,94 CHF	9.128,77 CHF	19 PC	9.609,24 CHF
1	1	4	14.059,55 CHF	13.356,59 CHF	702,97 CHF	18 PC	413,52 CHF
2	1	5	10.896,81 CHF	10.351,97 CHF	544,84 CHF	18 PC	375,75 CHF
3	1	6	11.754,06 CHF	11.166,36 CHF	587,70 CHF	14 PC	470,16 CHF
4	1	4	578.180,75 CHF	549.271,71 CHF	28.909,04 CHF	33 PC	25.041,26 CHF
5	1	5	402.498,63 CHF	382.373,70 CHF	20.124,93 CHF	27 PC	29.814,72 CHF
6	1	6	163.037,42 CHF	155.645,55 CHF	8.191,87 CHF	31 PC	10.570,16 CHF
1	1	4	11.157,42 CHF	10.376,40 CHF	781,02 CHF	14 PC	398,48 CHF
2	1	5	11.586,83 CHF	10.775,75 CHF	811,08 CHF	14 PC	362,09 CHF
3	1	6	14.498,10 CHF	13.483,24 CHF	1.014,86 CHF	14 PC	453,07 CHF
4	1	4	422.087,87 CHF	392.541,72 CHF	29.546,15 CHF	25 PC	33.767,02 CHF
5	1	5	359.131,77 CHF	333.992,54 CHF	25.139,23 CHF	25 PC	28.730,54 CHF
6	1	6	193.529,96 CHF	179.982,86 CHF	13.547,10 CHF	38 PC	10.165,76 CHF

Figure: Content of the Fact Table and the 3 Dimension Tables Product, Time, Sales

The three foreign keys in the fact table define a product, a sale and a time for each record, thus determining the coordinates of a cell in an OLAP cube. This cell contains the key figures – such as sales volume, discount or price.

While the fact table contains the transaction data, the tables with the individual analysis characteristics of the dimensions contain the master data. In reality, the number of dimensions often lies between 10 and 20, with each dimension containing 10-20 analysis characteristics in turn. If the models were created straightforwardly (that is, without any "peculiarities"), they will reuse as many dimensions as possible.

Database adepts will already have noticed that the dimension tables are not normalized. This means a certain data redundancy is intentionally stored in the dimension tables and controlled. This has a direct impact on the performance of a query.

In reality, a fact table contains the most data records by far – up to several million. Consequently, during queries, an SQL statement is executed that performs a join of the fact table via the dimension tables. The key factor here is the join sequence of the query.

The following example illustrates this situation. Assume we have the following data volumes in our star schema:

- Sales analysis fact table: 10,000,000 records

- Time dimension table: 5 years (60 months)

- Product dimension table: 1000 products

- Sales dimension table: 50 distribution channels

Example

An enduser wants to examine the sales in the first quarter of 2005 that were achieved through Internet sales for the "Apparel" division.

A database that applies the selection criterion Division = "Apparel" to the product table, thus joining the fact table, and only then processes the other dimension tables is much less efficient than a database that applies the selection criteria to the dimension tables first and then applies this comparatively small data volume to the fact table.

Pro / Cons

The following advantages arise from using a star schema:

- Simple, intuitive data models

- Low number of join operations

- Low number of database tables

- Low effort required for database maintenance

The following disadvantages apply:

- Poor response times when dimension tables are large

- Dimension tables are not normalized

- No portrayal of levels within the dimensions

Snowflake Schema

The disadvantages of the star schema can be eliminated by moving to a snowflake schema; however, it needs many more tables. The snowflake schema is an enhancement of the star schema in which the attributes of the dimension tables are arranged in levels.

To do so, the reciprocal relationships of the attributes are examined.

Each quarter consists of 3 months.	1:n relationship
Each year consists of 4 quarters.	1:n relationship
Sales are made through several sales offices.	1:n relationship
Sales are made through several distribution channels.	1:n relationship
Each sales organization has one sales manager.	1:1 relationship
A company code encompasses several countries.	1:n relationship
A country can have several sales offices.	1:n relationship
Each sales office supports a single country.	1:1 relationship
Each country has one national currency.	1:1 relationship

We can now refine our data model based on these statements. 1:n relationships are good candidates for dimension levels, while 1:1 relationships can be portrayed as dimension levels or attributes. This decision between attribute and dimension level is one of the freedoms in modeling.

Snowflake Schema

The following diagram shows our case study as a snowflake schema. You can see the hierarchies of the different dimensions. These hierarchies directly specify the aggregation levels that can be selected using drilldown and rollup with OLAP application tools.

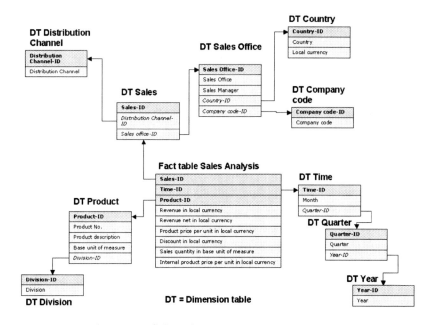

Figure: Case Study as Snowflake Schema

As the diagram shows, there are two parallel dimension levels: "distribution channel" and "sales office". This is because sales revenues are listed separately by distribution channel and sales office. This represents an n:m relationship that can only be modeled using a complex entity type, as each sales office uses different distribution channels, while the various distribution channels are used by multiple sales offices. The information as to which sales volume is achieved by each sales office and distribution channel is modeled using the "Sales" dimension.

Granularity, Aggregation, Aggregates

The term "granularity" describes the degree of detail of the data. Extremely detailed data has a low granularity; the greater the aggregation of the saved data, the greater the granularity [Inmon (1993a), p. 41]. Aggregation can take the form of totaling individual numeric data objects (key figures) or consolidation of several information objects to a new information object.

Determining and defining the granularity while taking the company's current and future situation in mind is a difficult task. Decision-makers would prefer a low granularity, as it facilitates extremely detailed analyses and evaluations. For the technical IT implementation, this would imply a high data volume and accordingly high memory requirements, along with the necessary IT resources to process these data volumes. This problem can be mitigated somewhat through a multi-layer granularity. In this approach, you define different degrees of granularity, with data aggregation increasing at each level.

You can define, for example, that the data from the current and past month has a very low granularity (such as sales volume at the level of individual sales orders per day), in order to enable detailed current analyses. At the end of the month, the data from the oldest month is summarized (aggregated) by totaling and/or average formation of the key figures at the weekly or monthly level. At the end of the quarter or year, you perform the corresponding aggregation at quarterly/annual level. The respective detailed data is archived. These aggregation runs – in which days are aggregated at the weekly level, weeks at the monthly level, and months at the annual level – are called "rolling aggregation".

The data can be aggregated at either the program or database level. Aggregation at the program level is performed during data transfer, by the transfer programs or corresponding programs in the data warehouse. At the database level, the aggregation rules are saved in the database system itself and activated through appropriate triggers after data transfer.

Investigations have shown that when a multi-level granularity is used, over 95% of the required analyses and evaluations use aggregates to access the data. Around 5% of the analyses have to access data at the detailed level [Inmon (1993c), p. 51]. Accordingly, the determination of aggregates – which results from an analysis of the expected query profile – is a major task. Due to the additional effort required to update and store the aggregates in the database, choosing which of the possible aggregates to pre-calculate is a crucial design decision.

Requirements of the Databases

The following requirements must be placed on all types of databases for a data warehouse:

- The data sources can be extremely heterogeneous: file systems, different SQL systems, other database systems, and so on

- In addition to conventional, record-oriented data types, it must also be possible to handle texts (substring search, neighboring search, ...), multimedia data (cross-referencing with other data) and spatial data (search for location in space, topological neighbors, and so on)

- In particular, optimizers must be able to find efficient strategies for the Cartesian product (join operator) and utilize the parallel processing options

- Different indexing techniques must be supported, especially since conventional B trees are not good at dealing with complex queries with a large number of attributes; bit lists are particularly interesting in this context

- Efficient techniques (hashing) and optimization have to be used to calculate multiple joins

- The handling of time must be included in both the data model and the indexing

II

Multi-Dimensional OLAP (MOLAP)

To obtain measurable performance gains with multi-dimensional data structures, it makes sense to save the data multi-dimensionally as well, in a multi-dimensional matrix. Multi-dimensional databases work on the assumption that all dimension combinations occur, and create the corresponding matrices "in advance" based on the cross product of all value ranges of the dimension objects. The address of each cell is then calculated from a simple chain of addition and multiplication, using the dimensional values and the size of each individual dimension element.

In general, the sum of the cells is calculated at loading time and then saved in separate cells.

Example

The following table which shows the revenues of our products sorted by countries serves as an example

Revenue in Q1.2005

Country	Product	Revenue
Germany	Street Bikes	450.000
Germany	Clothing	80.000
Switzerland	Moto Bike	270.000
France	Services	150.000
France	Street Bikes	230.000
France	Moto Bike	200.000
Italy	Fun Bike	350.000
Italy	Technic	100.000
Belgium	Helmets	50.000
Netherland	Technic	120.000
Netherland	Street Bikes	140.000

Figure: Starting Table with customer revenues by regions

Sparsely Populated Matrix

When we transfer the sales data from this table to a multi-dimensional matrix with the dimension objects "Country" (number: 6) and "Product" (number: 7), a 6x7 matrix with 42 cells would have to be provided in this case. Because the countries and products do not appear multiple times, only 11 cells actually contain a value, although the multi-dimensional data matrix provides a cell for each dimension element. The other cells contain a special NA (not available) value, to indicate that no analysis-relevant values are present. This case is described as a sparsely populated matrix (see next diagram).

Revenue in Q1.2005
Product ──────►

Country	Street Bikes	Moto Cross	Fun Bikes	Technic	Services	Clothing	Helmets	Sum
Germany	450.000	NA	NA	NA	NA	80.000	NA	530.000
Switzerland	NA	270.000	NA	NA	NA	NA	NA	270.000
France	230.000	200.000	NA	NA	150.000	NA	NA	580.000
Italy	NA	NA	350.000	100.000	NA	NA	NA	450.000
Belgium	NA	NA	NA	NA	NA	NA	50.000	50.000
Netherlands	140.000	NA	NA	120.000	NA	NA	NA	260.000
	820.000	470.000	350.000	220.000	150.000	80.000	50.000	2.140.000

Figure: Sales Table as Sparsely Populated Matrix

Densely Populated Matrix

The other extreme is a fully occupied matrix – that is, all the cells are populated with values.

Revenue in Q1.2005
Product ───────▶

Country	Street Bikes	Moto Cross	Fun Bikes	Technic	Services	Clothing	Helmets	Sum
Germany	450.000	390.000	100.000	90.000	100.000	80.000	40.000	1.250.000
Switzerland	200.000	270.000	90.000	30.000	70.000	40.000	20.000	720.000
France	230.000	200.000	190.000	110.000	150.000	90.000	50.000	1.020.000
Italy	180.000	320.000	350.000	100.000	140.000	70.000	10.000	1.170.000
Belgium	210.000	150.000	80.000	67.000	85.000	50.000	50.000	692.000
Netherlands	140.000	180.000	110.000	120.000	110.000	70.000	60.000	790.000
	1.410.000	1.510.000	920.000	517.000	655.000	400.000	230.000	5.642.000

Figure: Densely Populated Matrix

Summary

Actual multi-dimensional datasets usually lie somewhere between these two extremes.

To achieve better performance and save storage space, multi-dimensional databases require special procedures for dealing with sparsely populated matrices at the physical level. The relative performance benefits decline as the number of dimensions and dimension elements increases.

A manufacturing company with 25,000 customers and 1,000 products will require a dataspace with 250,000 cells. Each additional dimension increases the number of cells by the multiple of the elements it contains – for example, a person dimension with 200 elements would increase the above 250,000 cells 200-fold.

IV

SAP BW Basics

This chapter deals with several basic aspects of the SAP Business Information Warehouse. We intentionally follow the principle "as little as possible, as much as necessary". SAP BW has matured in recent years, adding a wide range of new functions whose description would go far beyond the scope of this book. We therefore recommend sources of additional information in the Appendix.

The sections below contain rough descriptions of the system architecture, the system data storage components, the data retrieval process, and tools for data utilization. The chapter concludes with a look at SAP Business Content, which provides preconfigured information models.

System Architecture

As a core component of SAP NetWeaver, the SAP Business Information Warehouse (SAP BW) provides data warehousing functionality, a business intelligence platform, and a suite of business intelligence tools.

SAP BW is a data warehouse solution whose architecture is based on the general reference architecture for data warehouses. It includes all the components required for the data warehouse process, from functions for data extraction (extraction, transformation and load) and components for data storage to complex tools for analyses and reports. It also contains components with Customizing and administration tools.

The basic principle of a warehouse in general and the SAP Business Information Warehouse in particular is really quite simple. There is a central storage component (e.g. the InfoCube), which periodically receives data from various source systems and then saves it in prepared form. The analyses and reports are based largely on this data store.

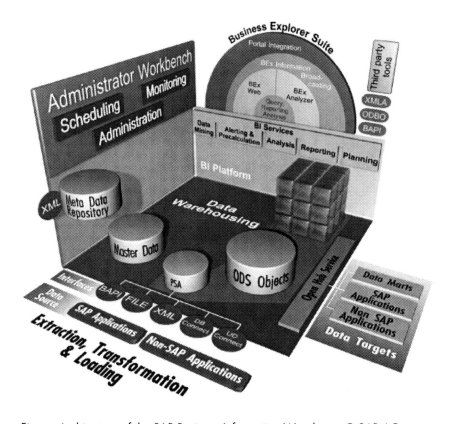

Figure: Architecture of the SAP Business Information Warehouse © SAP AG

The central architectural component the design and operation of a data warehouse is the Administrator Workbench. The elements of the SAP Business Information Warehouse are managed there, based on the consistent metadata. The Administrator Workbench is used to control, monitor and maintain the extraction and load process of the source data.

II

Data Storage Components in the BW

The data storage components mainly involve InfoObjects to set up the three-dimensional structures and to store master data, along with InfoProviders for saving transaction data.

InfoObjects

The smallest unit of data storage, upon which all other storage units are based, is the InfoObject. As such, they are considered to be the basic modules for storing data. They form the foundation of all InfoProviders, such as InfoCubes and objects from the Operational Data Store (ODS), which will be discussed in more detail in the next section.

Every InfoObject has a unique technical name, a specific data type and a specific length. InfoObjects are the smallest information units in SAP BW. They structure the information needed to create data targets.

Business evaluation objects are known in SAP BW as InfoObjects. They are divided into characteristics (for example, customers), key figures (such as sales volume), units (for example, currency, amount unit), time characteristics (for example, fiscal year) and technical characteristics (for example, request number).

Characteristics

Characteristics are terms of classification like company code, product, customer group, business year, period or region. Characteristics are supposed to have attributes, tests or hierarchies. If this is the case, we talk of characteristics with master data. Master data are data which remain unchanged over a longer period of time. They contain information which are used in the same way again and again. The characteristic "sales office", as an example, is supposed to have attributes like city, country, address etc. The sales office may have a (multilingual) textual description. Depending on the use case, several sales offices can have different hierarchical orders. For example, regional sales areas can be displayed in that way.

In all data targets, it can be referred to these master data. Consequently, the master data are stored only once in the system without redundancy.

Key figures

Key figures deliver the values which are to be analyzed in a query. It concerns quantities, amounts or numbers of pieces. The key figure determines further properties which influence both the load process and the view / display in the query. This includes the assignment of a currency or a unit of measure or the determination of the number of decimal places in the query. The system also provides conversion functionalities for the indication of values with currencies. Therefore, no difficulties arise if key figures with different currencies occur as the system converts them into a desired (target) currency according to different conversion versions.

Time Characteristics

Time characteristics are characteristics such as calendar day, calendar month, fiscal year, and so on. Transaction data always contains at least one time characteristic.

Units

Units are required to define properties of the key figures. Key figures of type amount are always assigned a currency key and key figures of type quantity also receive a unit of measurement.

Technical Characteristics

Technical characteristics merely have organizational relevance within SAP BW. An example of this is the request number in the InfoCube, which is generated for a data package when data is loaded, and helps to locate the data package in the InfoCube later.

InfoProviders

Any object that can be analyzed with an end-user tool can be called an InfoProvider. In SAP Business Explorer, this is one of the SAP BW reporting tools, which will be described in more detail later.

We differentiate between objects that actually contain data (InfoObjects, ODS objects and InfoCubes) and objects that merely communicate a view of the data. The latter involves objects whose data is saved in another system or in different physical objects. An example of this is the virtual InfoCube, which can display data from several different InfoCubes. This approach lets you analyze sales data and marketing data together, for example.

Primary Data Flow Objects

The most important elements of the data flow are explained below. Beginning from a source system, these elements are the Persistent Staging Area (PSA), the Operational Data Store (ODS) and, finally, the InfoCube. Whereas the PSA is merely temporary, the ODS and InfoCubes are used for permanent data storage.

Persistent Staging Area

The Persistent Staging Area is close to the source system, and serves as the initial store for transaction data, master data attributes, and texts. The data, which has not been transformed or modified yet, is saved here for further processing, and can also be subjected to a quality check, as the source data is saved in transparent tables. As a result, erroneous data can be changed or deleted at this point. The PSA also helps to improve the load performance, as the actual load step is detached from necessary transformation steps in further processing.

InfoCubes

InfoCubes can be considered to be the main storage objects and the central module for all reports and analyses in the Business Information Warehouse. Each InfoCube contains aggregated, reconciled data of a self-contained, delimited subject area. Their multi-dimensional data organization is tailored specifically to meet OLAP requirements.

We differentiate between several types of InfoCubes:

- BasicCubes store the data physically. The data is filled and updated through a periodic (daily, weekly, monthly, …) load operation.

- Transactional InfoCubes differ from Basic InfoCubes in their ability to support parallel write accesses. Basic InfoCubes are technically optimized for read accesses to the detriment of write accesses.

Transactional InfoCubes are used in connection with the entry of planning data.

- A RemoteCube is an InfoCube whose transaction data is managed externally, and not in the Business Information Warehouse. Only the structure of the RemoteCube is defined in SAP BW. The reporting data is read from another system. A RemoteCube lets you report on data in external systems, without having to store data physically in the data warehouse. You can, for example, include an external system from market data providers using a RemoteCube.

- An SAP RemoteCube is a RemoteCube that allows the definition of queries with direct access to transaction data in other SAP systems.

- Virtual InfoCubes are only logical views of a dataset. By definition, they are not data targets. From a reporting perspective, there is no difference to the BasicCube. You use virtual InfoCubes to analyze data from several BasicCubes together. You could, for example, analyze data from a sales InfoCube and data from a marketing InfoCube without having to store the data again (redundantly) in a common InfoCube.

Operational Data Store

The Operational Data Store saves merged, cleaned up transaction data from a variety of upstream systems at a detailed document level.

Unlike multi-dimensional data storage using InfoCubes, the data in ODS objects is stored in transparent, flat database tables. The cumulative update of key figures is supported for ODS objects, just as it is with InfoCubes, but with ODS objects it is also possible to overwrite data fields. This is particularly important with document-related structures, since changes made to documents in the source system do not apply solely to numeric fields such as order quantity, but also to non-numeric fields such as goods receiver, status, and delivery date. To map these changes in the BW ODS objects, the relevant fields in the ODS objects must also be overwritten and set to the current value.

III

Data Retrieval Process

The following diagram shows, among other things, an overview of the various data supply options. These options, as well as the data retrieval process, are described in more detail below.

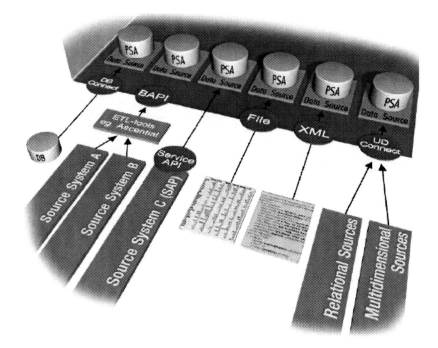

Figure: Data Supply and Data Retrieval Process © SAP AG

Data Sources

The source systems represent the starting point of the data loading process. A wide range of data sources can be used for data collection in SAP BW. The various options are described briefly below.

- Extraction from SAP systems: SAP BW features seamless integration with SAP applications. This integration is based on data extractors that are included in all standard SAP applications. A data extractor is a program with which data from the SAP source application can be retrieved (for goods movements in Materials Management, for example or sales orders from sales order management).

- Extraction from non-SAP systems: To enable the extraction of data from non-SAP sources at the application level, SAP BW has been equipped with an open interface, the staging BAPI (Business Application Programming Interface). This interface connects third-party applications with SAP BW.

- Extraction from databases: DB Connect offers functions for accessing individual tables or table views of a relational database. In addition, functions are available to simplify the loading of metadata by replicating metadata tables and views in the SAP BW metadata repository.

- Files: Data can also be loaded into SAP BW from two-dimensional ("flat") files, such as csv or ASCII format.

- XML: The XML format is increasingly becoming a standard for data interoperability. SAP BW uses an XML model based on the CWM (common warehouse metamodel) standard. XML files can be imported to or exported from SAP BW through the Administrator Workbench. An HTTP service is also available, which means metadata can be requested the same as on the Web server. The XML interface also supports a push mechanism, in which the data transfer is initiated from the source system to SAP BW.

DataSources

The data from the various source systems are made available to the Business Information Warehouse as DataSources. From a technical viewpoint, the DataSource encompasses a set of fields that logically belong together and that are offered for data transfer into SAP BW in a flat structure. The structure of a DataSource for SAP BW is called the transfer structure, and can be used for both master data and transaction data.

The data from a DataSource is transferred to SAP BW via the transfer structure upon request by SAP BW.

InfoSources

Logically related information is then grouped together to form a unit called an InfoSource. An InfoSource consists of a set of InfoObjects that form a flat structure, like the DataSource. This structure is called the communication structure. The special feature is that an InfoSource can take its data from different DataSources. If fields that logically belong together exist in various source systems, they can be grouped together into a single InfoSource in BW, in which multiple DataSources can be assigned to an InfoSource.

The data from the InfoSource is updated in the data targets. The data can be changed again during this process: The program routines that process the data in the InfoSource are called update rules.

The data loaded through the transfer structure is transformed using transfer rules. An extensive library of transformation functions that contain business logic can be used here to perform data cleansing and to make the data analyzable. The rules can be applied simply, without programming, by using formulas.

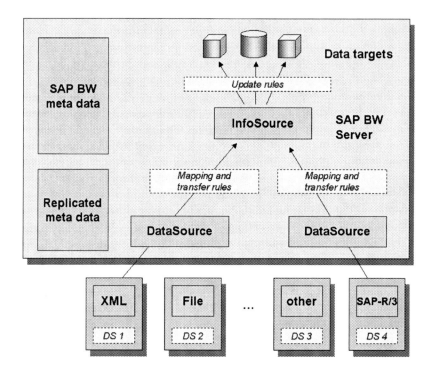

Figure: From DataSource to InfoSource

IV

Reporting and Analysis Tools

Several different SAP Business Explorer components are available for reporting and analysis purposes, along with a variety of third-party tools. This section only describes the former in detail, however.

The queries in the Business Information Warehouse form the foundation for all reports and analyses. All the front-end tools – including the Business Explorer Analyzer (BEx) – build on these queries. BEx is a plug-in for Microsoft Excel that adds OLAP-specific functions and data access to the SAP Business Information Warehouse. The OLAP processor of the BW system is the main data preparation component.

First, an InfoProvider upon which the query will be based, such as an InfoCube or ODS object, is located. The query is then created in the Query Designer, another SAP Business Explorer component. A further component is the Web Application Designer, which lets you create Web-based reporting applications. These applications form the foundation for executing analyses and reports in an HTML browser.

Third-party tools use the queries through a special, standardized interface that enables external access to the SAP system. This interface is comparable to the ODBC interface (which can be used to access various database systems), and is the de facto standard for accessing relational and/or multi-dimensional systems from various vendors: It is distributed by Microsoft and is abbreviated with "ODBO" (for "OLE DB for OLAP").

In turn, OLE DB for OLAP is short for Object Linking and Embedding DataBase for Online Analytical Processing.

V

Business Content

The term "Business Content" describes preconfigured, role-specific, task-specific information models in the SAP Business Information Warehouse. The Business Content is a particular strength of SAP's product compared to other vendors. The scope of these information models includes integral roles, workbooks, queries, InfoSources, InfoCubes, ODS objects, key figures, characteristics, update rules, and extractors for the SAP R/3 System. It also contains a variety of templates for Web-based reporting.

The modules are based on consistent metadata and are available immediately, enabling complex business analyses without requiring any additional programming effort. The Business Content is already custom-tailored to the needs of a variety of different users, and can be adapted to specific other needs with very little effort.

Use of the Business Content is especially effective in connection with other SAP components, such as SAP R/3 as the source system. It lets you start business intelligence projects quickly and cost-effectively. The Business Content is the foundation for analytics applications at a company: The enterprise reporting system is designed and set up on top of it.

Implementation with SAP BW 3.5

We use the Administrator Workbench to implement the case study in SAP BW. The Administrator Workbench is the tool for controlling, monitoring, and maintaining all of the processes connected with data staging and processing in the Business Information Warehouse.

In this part, we want to show how to ...

- ... create InfoObjects
- ... define InfoCubes
- ... transfer data from a DataSource to an InfoSource
- ... transfer data from an InfoSource to an InfoCube
- ... analyse data with the SAP Business Explorer Analyser

Choose the "Modeling" folder in the SAP menu and double-click the Administrator Workbench to start it.

I

InfoObjects

In the first part of this case study, we will first create InfoObjects.

InfoObjects

InfoObjects represent business (information) objects (such as articles or sales volume) that are generally divided into key figures and characteristics. They are the modules (structure components) for the multi-dimensional data model. InfoObjects map information in structured form, which is a prerequisite for constructing InfoCubes

Each InfoObject is saved in an InfoObject catalog, which in turn is assigned to an InfoArea. This storage structure resembles the storage of files in a file system.

Creating InfoAreas

We will first create an InfoArea to store our InfoObjects.

What Is an InfoArea?

InfoAreas are used to structure objects in SAP BW. Each object (such as InfoObject or InfoCube) is assigned to an InfoArea, whose structure is managed in the Administrator Workbench.

Therefore, InfoAreas are purely organizational tools, not for intended for reporting purposes. InfoAreas are usually named for the business application area for which the data warehouse application is being developed, for example, Sales, Production Planning, or Training.

InfoAreas can contain other InfoAreas.

Creating InfoAreas

For our case study, we want to create a new InfoArea called **Sales Case Study.** We will create two additional InfoAreas within this new InfoArea: one for the instructor and another for students.

Step 1

We open the **InfoObjects** area within the Administrator Workbench.

Modeling
⌖ InfoProvider
△ InfoObjects
◈ InfoSources
⊠ Source Systems
🗄 PSA

Figure: Start Editing InfoObjects © SAP AG

Step 2

You can open the context menu (right mouse button) on an InfoArea assigned to us to create additional InfoAreas.

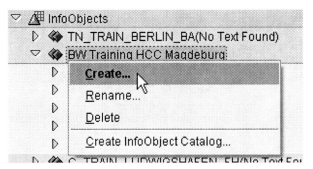

Figure: Create InfoArea via Context Menu © SAP AG

Step 3

We first create the **InfoArea** with technical name **MB1** and description **Sales Case Study.**

Create Application Components	
Application comp.	MB1
Long description	Sales Case Study

Figure: Create InfoArea © SAP AG

Step 4 and Step 5

We then create two more **InfoAreas** one level deeper: **MB1D** with description **Sales Case Study (Instructor)** and **MB1S** with description **Sales Case Study (Student).**

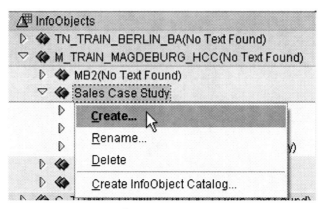

Figure: Create More InfoAreas © SAP AG

Our case study now has the required InfoArea structure.

Figure: InfoAreas for the Sales Case Study © SAP AG

Creating InfoObject Catalogs

The InfoObjects within an InfoArea are ultimately saved in an InfoObject catalog.

InfoObject Catalogs

An **InfoObject Catalog** is a collection of InfoObjects grouped according to application-specific criteria. We differentiate between key figures and characteristics that are used to set up the data models.

Creating an InfoObject Catalog

In the **Sales Case Study (Instructor)** info area, we create one InfoObject catalog each for key figures and characteristics.

Step 1

The **Create InfoObject Catalog** function is located in the context menu of the

InfoArea.

Figure: Create InfoObject Catalog © SAP AG

Step 2

Assign the technical name **MB1DK** and description **Key Figures (Instructor)** to the InfoObject catalog for key figures. Because key figures will be saved in the InfoObject catalog, you have to select InfoObject type Key Figure.

Figure: Create InfoObject Catalog for Key Figures © SAP AG

Step 3

We repeat the process to create the InfoObject catalog for the **characteristics** (technical name **MB1DM** and description **Characteristics (Instructor)**. Because characteristics will be stored in this InfoObject catalog, select **InfoObject type Characteristic**.

Creating Key Figures

We can now create the InfoObjects for key figures that we need for our case study.

Step 1

In the InfoObjects area, we first choose our InfoObject catalog for the key figures and choose the function for creating an InfoObject from the context menu.

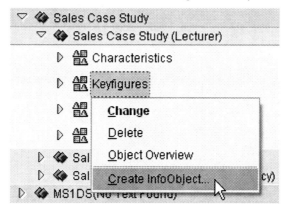

Figure: Create InfoObject © SAP AG

Step 2

We first create key figure **MB1DTPRIC** with description **Transfer Price in EUR**. Click  to confirm.

⌨ Create Key Figure	☒
⌨ KeyFig.	MB1DTPRIC
Long description	Transfer Price in Euro
Reference Key Figure	
Template	

Figure: Create InfoObject with Type Key Figure © SAP AG

Step 3

The key figure has type **Amount** and data type **CURR**. Choose **EUR** as the fixed currency.

Type/unit	Aggregation	Additional Properties

Type/data type
- ⦿ Amount   ○ Number   ○ Date
- ○ Quantity   ○ Integer   ○ Time

Data Type | CURR - Currency field, stored as

Currency/unit of measure

Fixed currency | EUR
Fixed Unit of Meas. |
Unit / currency |

Figure: Define the Data Type of the InfoObject © SAP AG

Step 4

You want to aggregate the key figure through totals creation. Define the aggregation as follows: The key figure will be aggregated as a **SUM** and involves a **Cumulative Value**.

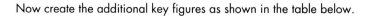

Figure: Define the Aggregation of the InfoObject © SAP AG

A **cumulative value** is a number that is measured over a period (that is, over an interval), such as sales or costs. Cumulative values can be logically aggregated over time. For example, you can add the sum of the daily sales volumes together to calculate the monthly sales volume. This aggregation type is called "totaling".

In contrast, non-cumulative values are reported for specific points in time, not periods (although information about a period is time-specific as well), such as the number of employees or warehouse stocks. Aggregation over time does not make sense for these values. It is useless to total figures such as "Units in Warehouse" over different periods, but it can be is useful to calculate the average, minimum, or maximum over the period.

Step 5

We now activate the key figure [i].

Now create the additional key figures as shown in the table below.

Key figure	Description	Data type	Currency/Unit
MB1DREVG	Gross sales volume	Curr	Currency/unit: 0CURRENCY

MB1DREVN	Net sales volume	Curr	Currency/unit: 0CURRENCY
MB1DPRICU	Price/unit in local currency	Curr	Currency/unit: 0CURRENCY
MB1DPCOSU	Product unit costs in EUR	Curr	Fixed currency: EUR
MB1DREBAT	Discount	Curr	Currency/unit: 0CURRENCY
MB1DQUAN	Quantity sold	Quan	Base unit of measure: 0BASE_UOM

Table: Create Key Figures

Creating Characteristics

We can now create the InfoObjects for characteristics that we need for our case study.

Creating Articles

Step 1

Click the right mouse button on **Characteristics (Instructor)** and choose **Create InfoObject...** in the context menu.

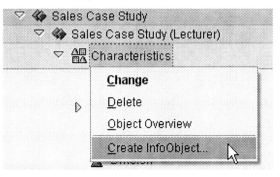

Figure: Create InfoObject © SAP AG

Step 2

Now assign the technical name **MB1DARTIC** and the description **Article**.

Figure: Create InfoObject Article © SAP AG

We will now define the properties attributes of the InfoObject in the **General tab** page.

Step 3

InfoObject **Article** is an object with a **Numeric Data Type** NUMC and has **Length 3.**

Figure: Define General Properties of a Characteristic © SAP AG

Step 4

You can use the **Business Explorer tab page** to configure whether the long or short name for this characteristic will be displayed in the Business Explorer, and whether it should only be displayed as **text** (e.g. "Scooter"), only as **key** (e.g. "001"), or with **key and text** together ("001 Scooter"). This definition serves as the default setting later in the Business Explorer.

General settings

Display	Text
Text Type	Default
BEx description	Short description
Selection	No Selection Restriction
Query Def. Filter Value Selection	Values in Master Data Table
Query Execution Filter Val. Selectn	Only Posted Values for Navigation
Currency attribute	
☐ AuthorizationRelevant	

Figure: Create Display of a Characteristic © SAP AG

Step 5

The Article characteristic will have both additional attributes, that means **master data,** and **texts**. Accordingly, set the checkboxes in the **Master Data/Texts tab page**.

General	Business Explorer	○ Master data/texts	Hierarchy	○ Attributes

☑ With master data		☑ With texts	
Master Data Tables		Text Table Properties	
View of MstrDtaTbls	/BIC/MMB1DARTIC	Text table	/BIC/TMB1DARTIC
Master data tab	/BIC/PMB1DARTIC	☑ Short text exists	
SID table attr.	/BIC/XMB1DARTIC	☐ Medium length text exists	
		☐ Long text exists	
		☑ Texts language dependent	
		☐ Texts are time-dep.	
☐ MstDataMaint with Authorizatio			

Figure: Create Characteristic with Master Data and Texts © SAP AG

Step 6

We assign the following **characteristics** as attributes to the **article:**

- Base unit of measure (0BASE_UOM)

- Division (0DIVISION)

- Transfer Price in EUR (MB1DTPRIC)

Figure: Assign Attributes to Article Characteristic © SAP AG

Some attributes merely have descriptive character, and are therefore not suitable as analysis characteristics; examples include the InfoObjects "First Name" and "Street". Analyzing the data of these characteristics would not make much sense in most cases.

We differentiate between:

- **Display attributes:** One example of this is the Base Unit of Measure attribute. This object is flagged as a mere display (DIS) attribute.

- **Navigation attributes:** In contrast, the Division attribute will be used to analyze data in the InfoCube, using OLAP functions. Accordingly, it has to be flagged as a navigation (NAV) attribute.

We use [icon] to activate or deactivate attributes as navigation attributes. When a navigation attribute is activated, an additional description for the navigation attribute can be specified. We will also call the navigation attribute "Division".

Step 7

Figure: Flag Attribute as Navigation Attribute or Display Attribute © SAP AG

Step 8

Finally we activate the InfoObject [⬜] and exit the definition of the InfoObject [⬆].

Creating Sales Offices

Repeat the above steps to create an InfoObject called **MB1DSALOF** with description **Sales Office**.

- The Sales Office InfoObject has **data type CHAR 4**-character.
- You want the Business Explorer to display the **Key and Text**.
- It has both **Master Data and Texts**.
- The attributes of the sales office are **Company Code** (0COMP_CODE) and **Country** (0COUNTRY).
- Both attributes will be used to analyze data with OLAP functions in the InfoCube, and therefore have to be activated as **Navigation Attributes**.

Figure: Create Characteristic Sales Area © SAP AG

As a result, each sales office is uniquely assigned to a company code and a country.

Again, we finally activate the InfoObject and exit the definition of the InfoObject ⬆.

Our case study also uses InfoObjects that we don't have to create ourselves, because they are already provided by SAP.

0COMP_CODE / Company code
0COUNTRY / Country key
0DIVISION / Division
0DISTR_CHAN / Distribution channel

Entering Master Data

In this section, we will manually create the master data for the sales offices first.

Step 1

To do so, choose **Maintain Master Data...** in the context menu of the sales office.

The **Maintain Master Data: Selection screen** appears. Confirm 🔄.

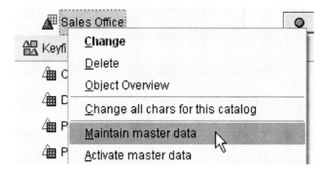

Figure: Enter Master Data © SAP AG

Step 2

Click the ⬜ symbol to maintain **new master data records**.

Characteristic MB1DSALOF - maintain master data: List

	Sales Office	Company code	Country	Descript.	

Figure: Maintain Master Data © SAP AG

Step 3

Create the master data for the sales offices according to the following table.

Sales Office	Company Code	Country	Description
1010	9000	DE	Hamburg
9000	9000	DE	Magdeburg
9100	9100	DE	Munich
9200	9100	CH	Montreux

Table: Create Master Data – Sales Office

Step 4

Now save your entries 💾 and examine the entered master data as a list, using the context menu of the InfoObject.

Characteristic MB1DSALOF - maintain master data: List

	Sales Office	Company code	Country	Descript.
	1010	9000	DE	Hamburg
	9000	9000	DE	Magdeburg
	9100	9100	DE	München
	9200	9200	CH	Montreux

Figure: Master Data of MB1DSALOF © SAP AG

Note

In most cases, master data is loaded from the operative source systems directly, using load programs. The load process is described in the later sections.

Creating Divisions

Step 5

Enter the following master data for InfoObject **Division** (0DIVISION)

Division	Language	Description
60	EN	Service
61	EN	Street Motorcycles
62	EN	Motocross
63	EN	Scooter

Table: Create Master Data – Sales Office

Create Company Codes

Step 6

Like in Step 5 above, we also have to **modify the Company Codes** (0COMP_CODE).

Company Code	Description (Medium)	Currency
9000	Motorsport Magdeburg AG	EUR
9100	Motorsport München GmbH	EUR
9200	Motorsport Montreux	CHF

Table: Create Master Data – Company Code

Creating Distribution
Channels

Step 7

Finally, we also have to modify the **Distribution Channels** (0DISTR_CHAN).

Distribution Channel	Description (Short)	Language
02	Wholesale trade	EN
03	Retail trade	EN
05	Internet	EN

Table: Create Master Data – Distribution channels

II

Defining InfoCubes

We will now create the InfoCube for the case study.

Step 1

We open the "InfoProviders" area within the Administrator Workbench.

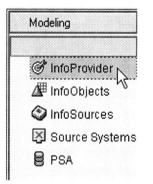

Figure: Editing InfoProviders © SAP AG

Creating InfoCubes

Like InfoObjects, InfoCubes are assigned to an InfoArea. The structure of the InfoAreas was generated when the InfoObjects were defined.

Step 2

Switch to the InfoArea for the case study and choose **Create InfoCube...** from the context menu.

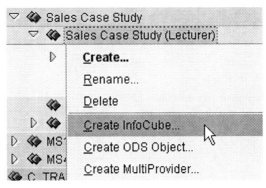

Figure: Create InfoCube © SAP AG

Step 3

Now assign the technical name **MB1DR01** and the description **Sales Motorsport AG**. Choose **BasicCube** as the InfoCube type.

Edit InfoCube

InfoCube	MB1DR01 — Sales Motorsport AG
InfoArea	MB1 — Sales Case Study

Copy from

InfoCube Type
- ● BasicCube
- ○ Virtual Cube
- ☐ Transactional

System Type (Namespace)
- ○ SAP (Delivered by SAP)
- ○ CUS (Generated by User)

Figure: Create InfoCube © SAP AG

A BasicCube is an InfoCube that is posted to directly using the update rules. In contrast, a RemoteCube is a virtual InfoCube whose data is managed externally, and not in the Business Information Warehouse.

Click ⬜ to create the InfoCube. The screen for defining the structure of the InfoCube appears.

Defining Characteristics

Step 4

We will now define the characteristics of the InfoCube.

On the right-hand side, all the available InfoObjects appear in the Template area. In our case, however, we only need the following characteristics: **Article, Distribution Channel,** and **Sales Office.**

We use the search help 🔍 to find the necessary InfoObjects easier. Because we already know that the characteristics we created all start with **MB1**, we enter this code together with an asterisk * – a wildcard that stands for any characters – in the search mask and click ✔ to start the search.

We select the appropriate lines in the template, click the arrow button to transfer them to the structure of our InfoCube, and then save 💾.

Figure: Copying Characteristics to the InfoCube © SAP AG

Time Characteristics

Step 5

We will now select the **time characteristics**. In doing so, we use the following characteristics predefined by SAP: **Calendar Year/Month**, **Calendar Month**, and **Calendar Year**.

Figure: Copying Time Characteristics to the InfoCube © SAP AG

Defining Key Figures

Step 6

In the next step, we select the key figures. We add **Price/Unit in Local Currency, Discount**, and **Gross Sales/Net Sales** to our InfoCube.

| Characteristics | Time characteristics | Key figures |

| AdFunction | Detail view | Units... |
| Template | InfoObject Catalog | <all InfoObjects> |

Structure				Template	
Key figure	Long description			Key figure	
MB1DPRICU	Price/unit in local currency		◀	0ABSNCE_HR	
MB1DQUAN	Quantity sold		▶	0ACCMPLRE...	
MB1DREBAT	Discount			0ACCPT_QTY	
MB1DREVG	Gross sales volume			0ACCRDFR_...	
MB1DREVN	Net sales volume			0ACC_QTY	
				0ACC_VALUE	

Figure: Copying Key Figures to the InfoCube © SAP AG

Defining Dimensions

Step 7

Now that we have copied the characteristics, time characteristics, and key figures to the structure of our InfoCube, we start the dialog for defining the dimensions in the "Characteristics" area.

| Characteristics | Time characteristics | Key figures |

| AdFunction | Detail view | Dimensions... | Nav.attributes... |
| Template | InfoObject Catalog | <all InfoObjects> | |

Figure: Create Dimensions © SAP AG

We first see a message stating that no dimensions have been created yet. Because no template is available in our case, we answer the question as to whether we want to create the dimensions from a template with "No".

Step 8

Define the two dimensions Product and Sales. The system assigns the technical IDs automatically.

Figure: Define Dimensions © SAP AG

Step 9

Now assign the **Article** characteristic to the **Product dimension** and the **Distribution Channel and Sales Office characteristics** to the Sales dimension.

This assignment involves three steps.

- First, select the characteristic ☑.
- Then position the cursor on the desired dimension.
- Lastly, assign the characteristic to the dimension.

Then click ✔ to exit the assignment function.

Figure: Assign Characteristics to the Dimensions © SAP AG

Navigation Attributes

We defined attributes when we defined the InfoObjects. The Division, for example, is an attribute of InfoObject **Article**, while Company Code and Country are attributes of InfoObject Sales Office.

When you define the InfoCube, you now have to determine which attributes you want to use as analysis objects in reporting and define them as navigation attributes. You do this in the "Navigation Attributes" area. If you do not define attributes as navigation attributes, they will merely be display attributes and cannot be used for data analysis.

Figure: define Navigation Attribute

Step 10

Use all the attributes for our case study .

Switch On/Off Navigation Attribute		
Structure		
Navigation attribute	Long description	I/O
MB1DARTIC__0DIVISION	Division	☑
MB1DSALOF__0COMP_CODE	Company code	☑
MB1DSALOF__0COUNTRY	Country key	☑

Figure: Navigation Characteristics © SAP AG

Step 11

You can now activate the InfoCube ⬜. The version and object status switch to active. In addition, a message appears in the status bar indicating the InfoCube is now active.

Displaying the Data Model

Step 12

In closing, now open the context menu of the InfoCube and display the data model.

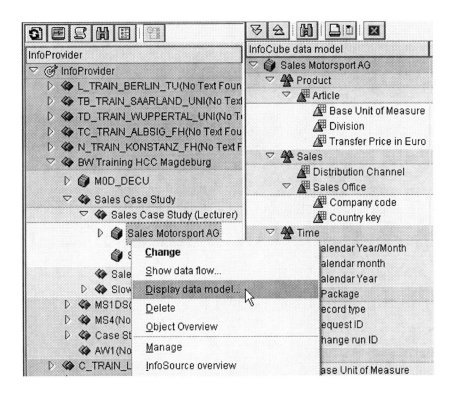

Figure: Display the Data Model of the InfoCube © SAP AG

III

Load Master Data

This section describes the load process for data from source systems.

Create Application Components

Like you created InfoAreas for the InfoProviders previously, you will now create application components for the InfoSources.

Application Components

Application components are used to structure InfoSources in SAP BW. Each InfoSource (such as InfoObject or InfoCube) is assigned to an application component, whose structure is managed in the Administrator Workbench.

The application component is strictly an organizational aid.

Application components can contain other application components.

Creating Application Components

For our case study, we want to create a new application component called **Sales Case Study**. We will create two additional application components within this new application component: one for the instructor and another for students.

Step 1

We open the "InfoSources" area within the Administrator Workbench.

Modeling
☀ InfoProvider
◢ InfoObjects
◈ InfoSources
⊠ Source Systems
⊟ PSA

Figure: Start Editing InfoSources © SAP AG

Step 2

You can open the context menu (right mouse button) on an application component assigned to us to create additional application components.

▽ ⊛ BW Training HCC Magdeburg
  ▷ | **Create...** ↖
  ▷ | Rename...
  ▷ | Delete
  ▷ | Create InfoSource...
  ▷ ⊛ Sales Case Study CS

Figure: Create Application Component via Context Menu © SAP AG

Step 3

We first create the application component with technical name ZMB1 and description **Sales Case Study.** Click ☑ to confirm.

Create Application Components

Application comp.	ZMB1
Long description	Sales Case Study

✓ ✗

Figure: Create Application Component © SAP AG

Step 4 and Step 5

We then create two more application components one level deeper: **ZMB1D** with description **Sales Case Study (Instructor)** and **ZMB1S** with description **Sales Case Study (Student)**.

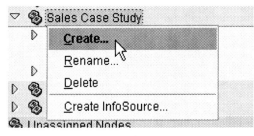

Sales Case Study

- Create...
- Rename...
- Delete
- Create InfoSource...

Unassigned Nodes

Figure: Create More Application Components © SAP AG

Our case study now has the required application component structure.

Sales Case Study	ZMB1
Sales Case Study (Lecturer)	ZMB1D
Sales Case Study (Students)	ZMB1S

Figure: Application Components for the Sales Case Study © SAP AG

Loading Master Data

Because the master data for the **Article** characteristic is rather complex, it is loaded directly from a source system. To illustrate this process, a delimiter-separated data file is used as a source system.

```
MB1DARTIC_ATTR.csv - Editor
Datei  Bearbeiten  Format  Ansicht  ?
MB1DARTIC;0BASE_UOM;0DIVISION;MB1DTPRIC
1;PC;63;1.810,00
2;PC;61;6.500,00
3;PC;62;5.800,00
4;PC;60;0
5;PC;60;0
6;PC;60;0
```

Figure: Data File with Attributes

Because our InfoObject Article has multi-lingual texts, they also have to be loaded from a file.

```
MD1DARTIC_TEXT.csv - Editor
Datei  Bearbeiten  Format  Ansicht  ?
Product;Language;Text
1;DE;Roller;
1;EN;Motorbike;
1;FR;Cyclomoteur;
2;DE;Straßenmotorrad;
2;EN;Motorcycle;
2;FR;Moto;
3;DE;Motocross;
3;EN;Motocross;
3;FR;Motocross
4;DE;Bekleidung;
4;EN;Clothing;
4;FR;Habillement;
5;DE;Helme;
5;EN;Helmets;
5;FR;Casques;
6;DE;Technik;
6;EN;Technics;
6;FR;Technique
```

Figure: Data File with Texts

Creating InfoSources

Step 1

We first create an InfoSource. To do so, we switch to the application component of our case study and choose the Create InfoSource function from the context menu.

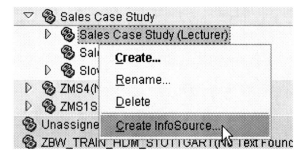

Figure: Create InfoSource © SAP AG

Defining the Update Type

Step 2

Select the Direct Update of master data and assign the technical name **MB1DARTIC**.

Note

Direct update means that the master data of an InfoObject is updated unchanged from the InfoSource in a master data table, without any options for manipulating the data.

When an InfoSource has flexible updating, update rules are used to load the data from the communication structure into the data targets (InfoCubes, ODS objects, master data).

Create InfoSource

○ Flexible Update in any Data Target (Except Hierarchies)

InfoSource	
Long description	
Template-InfoSource	

◉ Direct Update of Master Data

InfoObject	MB1DARTIC

✔ ✖

Figure: Direct Update © SAP AG

Step 3

Confirm your entries and the subsequent messages ✔.

We then examine the field structure of the generated InfoSource, and remember the structure of our InfoObject for article MB1DARTIC. The object key is the first field in the communication structure, followed by the attributes of the InfoObject.

Communication Structure

InfoObject	Descript.	S.	Type	Length	Deci...	Unit	Field	
MB1DARTIC	Article	▲	NU...	3	0		/BIC/MB1DAR...	
0BASE_UOM	Base Unit	▲	UNIT	3	0		BASE_UOM	
0DIVISION	Division	▲	CH...	2	0		DIVISION	
MB1DTPRIC	Transfer Price	▦	CU...	17	2		/BIC/MB1DTP...	

Figure: InfoSource Communication Structure © SAP AG

Assigning the DataSource

Step 4

We will now assign the DataSource to the InfoSource.

Figure: Assign DataSource © SAP AG

Step 5

We assign source system **PC_FILE** as the DataSource for InfoSource **MB1DARTIC**. Then click ✅ to save.

☞ Master Data - InfoSource : Assign Source System	
InfoSource	MB1DARTIC
Source system	PC_FILE

Figure: Assign PC_FILE as Source System © SAP AG

Creating the Transfer Structure Fields

As a result of the direct update, you can now generate all the programs that are required to load the data into the data targets.

1. All the data fields as they were created in the InfoObject.

2. The attributes of the InfoObject are loaded first, followed by the texts. This means the system creates two DataSources (attributes and texts). This separation of attributes and descriptive texts makes multi-lingual descriptions possible.

The system automatically switches to the editing function for the transfer structure. We verify that the InfoObjects are shown exactly in the sequence in which they are specified in the customer file.

Figure: DataSource Transfer Structure © SAP AG

Step 6

We now activate the transfer rules ⬚.

Displaying the Preview

Step 7

Activate the file preview. Click ⬚ to activate the preview function.

Figure: Activate the Preview © SAP AG

We first have to define the parameters for the preview.

1. Our source file is a csv file.

2. The first row of our file contains the column names. To prevent this header from being transferred, we have to specify the number of header lines to ignore as "1".

3. If a large number of records is involved, it makes sense to limit the number of lines to display in the preview.

4. Specify the file name as the path to the file from which you want to upload the data.

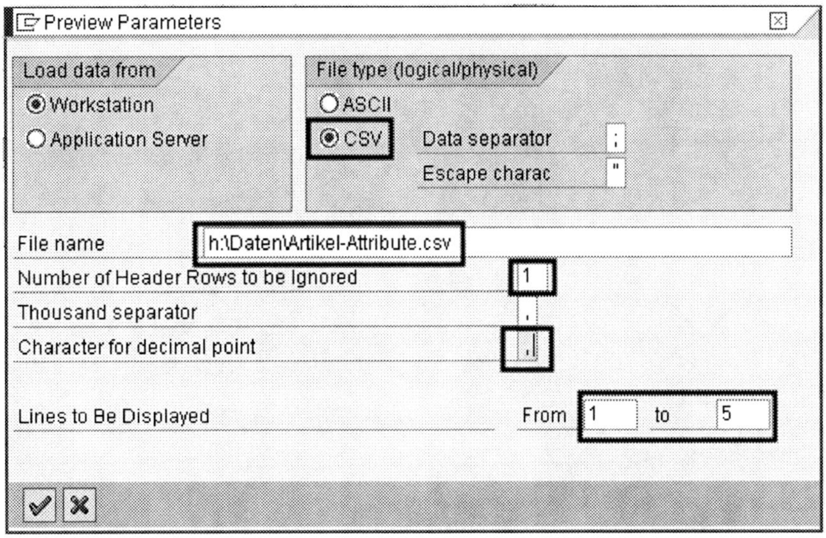

Figure: Configure Preview © SAP AG

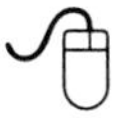

Step 8

Click to display the preview.

Rec.no.	Product	Base Unit	Division	Price in E
1	001	PC	63	1810.00
2	002	PC	61	6500.00
3	003	PC	62	5800.00
4	004	PC	60	0.00
5	005	PC	60	0.00

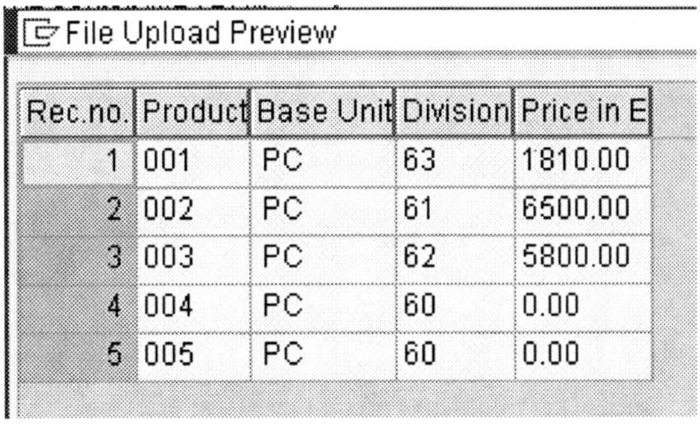

Figure: File Preview © SAP AG

Creating InfoPackages

Step 1

Create an InfoPackage for DataSource PC_File of our InfoSource.

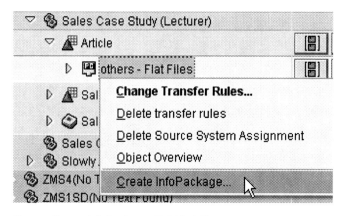

Figure: Create InfoPackage © SAP AG

Step 2

Because the system determines the technical name automatically, you merely enter a description, choose the master data as the DataSource, and save the settings.

DataSource		
Name	Technical Name	Data Type for the DataSo
Product (Master Data)	MB1DARTIC_ATTR	Master data attribute
Product (Texts)	MB1DARTIC_TEXT	Texts

BW InfoSource — Article — MB1DARTIC
Source system — others - Flat Files — PC_FILE

InfoPackage Description — Article load master data

Figure: Define InfoPackage © SAP AG

Step 3

We now have to define the parameters for previewing the external data.

1. Specify the file name as the path to the file from which you want to upload the data.

2. Our source file is a csv file. The columns are separated by semicolons.

3. The first row of our file contains the column names. To prevent this header from being transferred, we have to specify the number of header lines to ignore as "1".

Figure: Scheduler: Load External Data © SAP AG

Step 4

We choose to write the data directly to the InfoObject.

Figure: Scheduler: Processing © SAP AG

PSA stands for "persistent staging area". If this button is set, a database table is generated based on the transfer structure. The data is then saved in the table. If the button is not selected, the data is transported directly to the InfoObject.

Step 5

Now start processing the data.

Figure: Scheduler: Scheduling © SAP AG

Step 1

After the "Data was requested" message, we switch to the monitor.

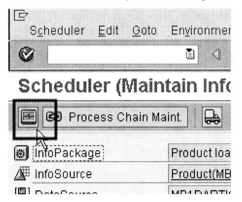

Figure: Starting the Monitor © SAP AG

Step 2

There we see that our request arrived properly.

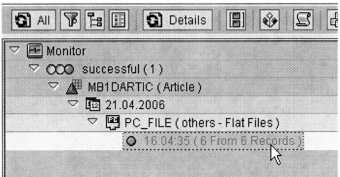

Figure: Monitor

Step 3

Click the icon to exit the monitor.

Loading Texts for Master
Data

We proceed analogous to creating the InfoPackage for the texts.

InfoPackage Description	Article load text	

DataSource		
Name	Technical Name	Data Type for the DataSc
Product (Master Data)	MB1DARTIC_ATTR	Master data attribute
Product (Texts)	MB1DARTIC_TEXT	Texts

Figure: Create InfoPackage Texts © SAP AG

InfoSources Overview

The following diagram once again shows the objects that were generated to load master data.

1. Application components for the sales case study

2. InfoSource for InfoObject "Article"

3. DataSource for DataSource "Article"

4. InfoPackage for attributes

5. InfoPackage for texts

▽ 🏷 Sales Case Study		**1**		ZMB1
▽ 🏷 Sales Case Study (Lecturer)				ZMB1[
▽ 🔩 Article	**2**		📇 📮	MB1D,
3 ▽ 🖳 others - Flat Files			📇 📮	PC_FI
4 ⚙ Article load master data			📇	ZPAK_
5 ⚙ Article load text			📮	ZPAK_

Figure: InfoSources Overview © SAP AG

128

IV

Load Transaction Data

In this section, we will now prepare the transaction data for loading into the InfoCube. To do so, we first create an InfoSource for sales data.

Creating InfoSources

Step 1

Once again, we first create an InfoSource. To do so, we switch to the application component of our case study and choose the Create InfoSource function from the context menu.

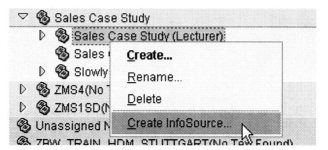

Figure: Create InfoSource © SAP AG

Defining the Update Type

Step 2

This time, we do not select direct update but flexible update (because we want to make several calculations), and assign technical name MB1DS0001 and description "Sales Data Motorsport AG".

```
┌ Create InfoSource
│
│ ◉ Flexible Update in any Data Target (Except Hierarchies)
│     InfoSource              MB1DS0001
│     Long description        Sales data Motorsport AG
│     Template-InfoSource     
│
│ ○ Direct Update of Master Data
│     InfoObject               
│
│ ✔ ✖
```

Figure: Create InfoSource © SAP AG

Define the InfoSource with flexible update ✔ and confirm the status message indicating that the InfoSource was created successfully.

Assigning the DataSource

Step 3

Now open the context menu and assign a DataSource to InfoSource "Sales Data Motorsport AG". Specify PC_FILE as the source system and click Adopt ✓.

▷ 🗇 Sales Data Motorsport AG

🦋 Sales C	**Change**
> 🦋 Slowly ₂	Rename...
🦋 ZMS4(No T	Show data flow...
🦋 ZMS1SD(N	Delete
Inassigned N	Object Overview
BW_TRAIN_H	
UH_TRAIN_N	Assign DataSource... ᨀ
TH_TRAIN_M	Delete communication structure
Q_TRAIN_DA	Create SAP remote InfoCube...
TL_TRAIN_L(	

Figure: Assign DataSource © SAP AG

Confirm the message indicating the DataSource assignment to the InfoSource.

Creating the Transfer Structure Fields

Step 4

We will now define the fields of the DataSource. To do so, we enter the InfoObjects as data fields of the transfer structure in the column of the InfoObject.

Caution

It is essential that you adhere to the field sequence in the transfer structure, as it corresponds to the format of our data file.

Technical Name	Description
MB1DSALOF	Sales office
MB1DARTIC	Article
ODISTR_CHAN	Distribution channel
ODISTR_CHAN	Calendar year/month
MB1DQUAN	Quantity sold
MB1DREVG	Gross sales volume
MB1DREBAT	Discount

Table: InfoObjects in the Transfer Structure

Note

The field sequence can be changed manually later. To do so, first select the row you want to move, place the cursor in front of where you want to insert the line, and press the "Move to Cursor Position" button .

Figure: Edit Transfer Structure © SAP AG

Please note again that the field sequence in the transfer structure has to correspond to the sequence in the flat file (0BASE_UOM after MB1DQUAN, 0CURRENCY after MB1DREVG).

The system adds the units 0BASE_UOM (Base Unit of Measure) and 0CURRECY (Currency) automatically, because these objects were specified as unit and currency, respectively, during the definition of the InfoObjects.

133

Figure: The Base Unit of Measure is Added Automatically © SAP AG

Step 5

Now save your settings 💾.

Creating the Communication Structure Fields

We will now transfer the fields from the transfer structure of the DataSource to the communication structure of the InfoSource.

Step 6

To do so, first expand the communication structure menu 🔄. All the fields in the InfoSource are displayed on the right, for transfer to the communication structure.

Select all the InfoObjects and click ⏪ to copy them to the communication structure of the InfoSource.

🔄 Communication_Struct.				
Status	Active			

Communication Structure

InfoObject	Descript.	St	R..	Chec
0BASE_UOM	Base Unit		☐	
0CALMONTH	Calendar Y..		☐	
0CURRENCY	Currency		☐	
0DISTR_CHAN	Distribution		☐	
MB1DARTIC	Article		☐	
MB1DQUAN	Quantity sold		☐	
MB1DREBAT	Discount		☐	
MB1DREVG	Gross sale..		☐	
MB1DSALOF	Sales Office		☐	
MB1DREVN	Net sales v..		☐	

Template MB1DS0001

ISource fields

InfoObject	Field	S..	Type	Lengt
0BASE_UOM	BASE_UOM		UNIT	3
0CALMONTH	CALMONTH		NU..	6
0CURRENCY	CURRENCY		CU..	5
0DISTR_CH..	DISTR_CH..		CH..	2
MB1DARTIC	/BIC/MB1DA..		NU..	3
MB1DQUAN	/BIC/MB1D..		QU..	17
MB1DREBAT	/BIC/MB1D..		CU..	17
MB1DREVG	/BIC/MB1D..		CU..	17
MB1DREVN	/BIC/MB1D..		CU..	17
MB1DSALOF	/BIC/MB1D..		CH..	4

Figure: Copying InfoObjects to the Communication Structure © SAP AG

Step 7

We now want to extend the communication structure with an additional InfoObject, the Net Sales Volume. We will calculate the net sales volume later. To do so, we first enter the technical name of the InfoObject (MB1DREVN) in the communication structure and press Enter to confirm. The InfoObject is then added to the communication structure.

MB1DREVG	Gross sale...				▶	MB1DREVG	/BIC/MB1D...	CU...	17
MB1DSALOF	Sales Office				▶▶	MB1DREVN	/BIC/MB1D...	CU...	17
MB1DREVN:	t sales v...					MB1DSALOF	/BIC/MB1D...	CH...	4

Figure: Extended Communication Structure of the InfoSource © SAP AG

Step 8

In conclusion, save the InfoSource again, just to be sure.

Defining the Transfer Rules

Step 9

We switch back to the transfer structure and see that the status display of the transfer rules changes to yellow.

Transfer_Structure/Transfer_Rules

			Transfer Method
Source System	PC_FILE - others - Flat Files (X)		⦿ 🖫 PSA
DataSource	MB1DS0001 - Sales data Motorspor...		○ 🖫 IDoc
Status	Modified(Save...	Create DS	Assign DS

DataSource/Trans. Structure   Transfer Rules

Figure: Status Display of Transfer Rules © SAP AG

The programs that transfer the data from the transfer structure of the DataSource to the communication structure of the InfoSource are called transfer rules.

We now have to define how the field we just added to the communication structure, MB1DREVN "Net Sales Volume", will be supplied with data. The Net Sales Volume is calculated as the Gross Sales Volume minus the Discount.

Step 10

We first switch to the menu for editing transfer rules.

	MB1DREBAT	←	⚠	MB1DREBAT	/BIC/
	MB1DREVG	←	⚠	MB1DREVG	/BIC/
	MB1DSALOF	←	⚠	MB1DSALOF	/BIC/
	MB1DREVN	←	✖		/BIC/

Figure: Edit Transfer Rules © SAP AG

Step 11

Then choose the "Formula" radio button, click "Create" ☐ and in the next step, assign the name "Calculate Net Sales" to the formula.

Transfer rules

- ○ ⚠ InfoObject
- ○ 🕐 Constant
- ○ 📄 Routine
- ● 📊 Formula

ℹ Transformation Library

Figure: Create Formula © SAP AG

After confirmation, ✓ the formula editor is displayed.

Step 12

You now select the components of the formula by double-clicking on InfoObject Gross Sales Volume, the operator (subtraction), and InfoObject Discount, and then make sure the formula syntax is correct .

Form. Calculate Net Sales (MB1DREVN) Create

Gross sales volume - Discount

Show me: All Fields

Type	Field	Name	Data Type	Length
	/BIC/MB1DARTIC	Sales Item	NUMC	3
	/BIC/MB1DQUAN	Quantity	QUAN	17
	/BIC/MB1DREBAT	Discount	CURR	17
	/BIC/MB1DREVG	Gross sales volume	CURR	17
	/BIC/MB1DSALOF	Sales Office	CHAR	4
	BASE_UOM	Base Unit	UNIT	3
	CALMONTH	Calendar Year/Month	NUMC	6
	CURRENCY	Currency	CUKY	5
	DISTR_CHAN	Distribution Channel	CHAR	2
	CVST_DATLO	Local data	DATS	8

Figure: Create Formula in Formula Editor © SAP AG

Click [icon] to return to the transfer rule and confirm the settings [✔].

Step 13

The status of the transfer rules now changes to green, and we can activate the programs for transferring the data from the transfer structure to the communication structure [icon].

Displaying the Preview

Step 14

Click the symbol in the transfer structure to go to the preview.

Figure: Activate the Preview © SAP AG

Again, we first have to define the parameters for the preview.

1. Our source file is a csv file.

2. Specify the file name as the path to the file from which you want to upload the data. The file with the sales data is called "SalesData.csv".

3. The first row of our file contains the column names. To prevent this header from being transferred, we have to specify the number of header lines to ignore as "1".

4. We also have to specify that our source file uses . as thousands separators and , as decimal points.

5. Lastly, limit the number of lines to be displayed.

Figure: Preview Parameters © SAP AG

Once all the parameters have been configured, click to start the preview.

Figure: View of Transaction Data in the Preview © SAP AG

What Now?

We now exit the preview. In the next step, we will write the data from the InfoSource to the InfoCube.

V

From InfoSource to InfoCube

This section describes how transaction data is loaded into the InfoCube.

Defining the Data Flow

We now want to load the transaction data into the InfoCube.

Update Rules

As we selected the option flexible update for our InfoSource MB1DS0001, we can now use update rules which describe the transformation of data from InfoSource to InfoCube. The following example will help emphasize this.

Step 1

Open the context menu InfoProvider and choose **Create Update Rules...**

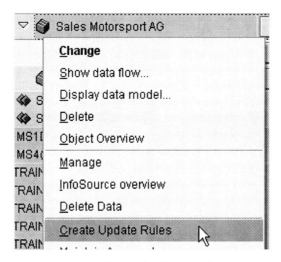

Figure: Create Update Rules © SAP AG

Assigning the InfoSource

Step 2

Specify our InfoSource **MB1DS0001** as the **data source for the sales data** and press **Enter** to confirm.

The system tells you that it was not able to determine suitable fields from the InfoSource for all of the key figures in the InfoCube, and these key figures have therefore been set to "No Update".

Click to create the rules.

Defining a Formula

We now map the fields of the InfoSource to the key figures in the InfoCube.

Step 3

The system was not able to determine any suitable fields from the InfoSource for the "Price/Unit in Local Currency" – the reason fro the above message – so we will now create a formula.

	Create Start Routine			🔁		🔲 🗂
Update Rules						
Status	Key Figures		Ty.	Srce Fields		
◇	Price/unit in local currency		✖			▲
●	Quantity sold	←	⊞	Quantity sold		▼
◐	Discount	←	⊞	Discount		

142

Figure: Mapping the Key Figures of the InfoCube © SAP AG

Step 4

To do so, first select update type "Addition" and then choose the "Formula" radio button as the update method.

Figure: Create Formula 1 © SAP AG

Step 5

Click the ⬜ symbol to create the formula; enter the description "Sales Volume".

Step 6

Define the key figure:

Price per unit in local currency := IF(Quantity sold <> 0, Gross Sales Volume / Quantity sold, 0)

Form. Sales Volume (MB1DPRICU) Create

```
IF( Quantity sold <> 0, Gross sales volume / Quantity sold, 0 )
```

Show me: All Fields

Type	Field	Name	Data Type	Length
	/BIC/MB1DARTIC	Article	NUMC	3
	/BIC/MB1DQUAN	Quantity sold	QUAN	17
	/BIC/MB1DREBAT	Discount	CURR	17
	/BIC/MB1DREVG	Gross sales volume	CURR	17
	/BIC/MB1DREVN	Net sales volume	CURR	17
	/BIC/MB1DSALOF	Sales Office	CHAR	4

/	+
-	*
(	)

=	<
<>	<=

| And | Or |

Figure: Create Formula 3 © SAP AG

Then click to return to the update.

Step 7

We now have to define the unit in which the key figure Price/Unit in Local Currency will be displayed. In our case, this is the same unit that was assigned to InfoObject Gross Sales Volume, namely 0CURRENCY

Target Unit	Source Unit
Currency key	⬅ Currency key

Translation

○ No Currency Translation

Figure: Define Unit © SAP AG

We now see that an update rule with type Formula has been created for key figure Price/Unit in Local Currency.

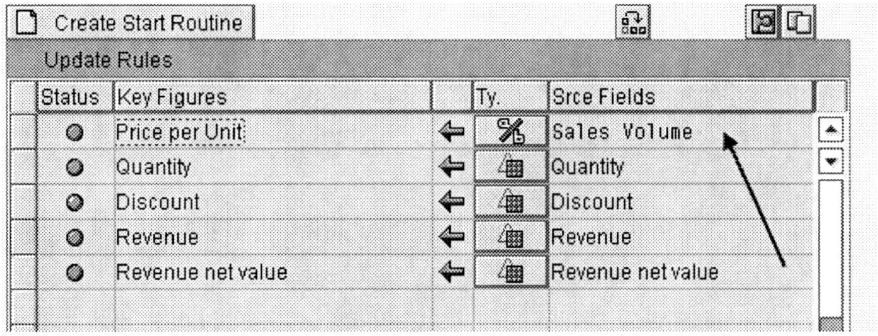

Figure: Create Update Rules © SAP AG

Save the update rules ⊞ and click Details ⊡ to maintain the characteristics.

Defining Characteristics

Step 8

We now map the fields of the InfoSource to the characteristics in the InfoCube.
As you can see in the diagram below, the fields in the communication structure of
the InfoSource have been mapped to the characteristics of the InfoCube without
changes.

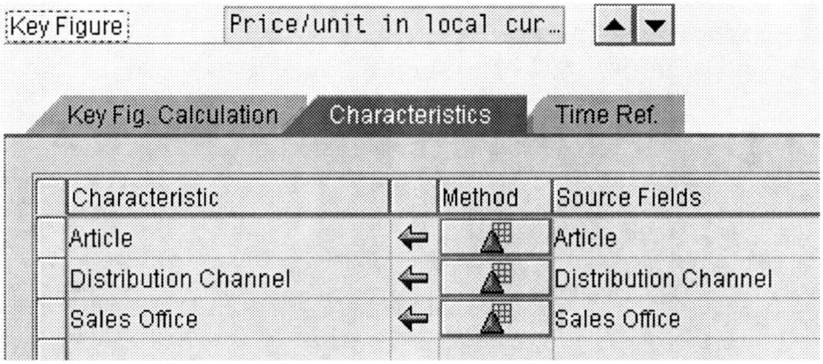

Figure: Update Rules of Characteristics © SAP AG

Defining Time
Characteristics

Step 9

We now map the time characteristics of the InfoSource to the time characteristics in the InfoCube. As we see in the diagram, the time characteristics "Calendar Month" and "Calendar Year" are derived correctly and automatically from the characteristic of the InfoSource (source field) "Calendar Year/Month" through the update rules.

Key Fig. Calculation	Characteristics		Time Ref.		

Time Characteristic		Method	Source Fields	Auto...	
Calendar Year/Month	←	⊞	Calendar Year/Month		▲ ▼
Calendar month	←	⊞	Calendar Year/Month	✓	
Calendar Year	←	⊞	Calendar Year/Month	✓	

Figure: Update Rules of Time Reference © SAP AG

Generating the Update

We now have to generate the programs that will transfer the data from the InfoSource to the InfoCube.

We do so by activating the update rules [I].

Loading Data from the File to the InfoCube

Now that we have created the update rules, we want to load the data from the csv file to the InfoCube. To do so, we switch to the "InfoSource" area in the Administrator Workbench and first create an InfoPackage for the sales data.

Step 1

We open the context menu of DataSource "PC_FILE" and then choose **Create InfoPackage...**

Sales Data Motorsport AG

▽ ◈ Sales Data Motorsport AG

▷ 🖳 others - Flat Files

🦕 Sal **Change Transfer Rules...**

▷ 🦕 Slo **Delete transfer rules**

🦕 ZMS4(I **Delete Source System Assignment**

🦕 ZMS1S **Object Overview**

Jnassigne

BW_TRAI **Create InfoPackage...**

UH_TRAIN_MOENSTER_UNI(No Text Found)

Figure: Create InfoPackage © SAP AG

Step 2

The system determines the technical name automatically. Enter the description "**Load Sales Data**" for the **InfoPackage** and then **save**.

Step 3

Once again, we define the parameters for the preview.

1. Specify the file name as the path to the file from which you want to upload the data. The file with the sales data is called "Salesdata.csv".

2. Our source file is a csv file.

3. We also have to specify that our source file uses . as thousands separators and , as decimal points.

4. The first row of our file contains the column names. To prevent this header from being transferred, we have to specify the number of header lines to ignore as "1".

Figure: Describe External Data © SAP AG

Step 4

In the "Processing" tab, the system has set field "PSA and then into Data Targets" by default. We only want to update the data in the PSA (persistent staging area) at first, however, so we set the radio button to "Only PSA".

Figure: Update of Data in the Persistent Staging Area © SAP AG

Step 5

You can now see your InfoCube in the Data Targets tab. Use the suggestion of updating the data in all data targets for which active rules exist.

		Data Selection	External data	Processing	**Data Targets**	Update

◉ Update in All Data Targets for Which Active Rules Exist
◯ Select Data Targets

U...	D...	Data Target Name	M...	M...	A...	D...	Technical name
☐	🎁	Sales Motorsport AG	✕	🖊		☐	MB1DR01

Figure: Data Targets © SAP AG

If the InfoCube doesn't appear, this means the update rules are missing or haven't been activated yet.

Step 6

Finally, start the load process in the "Schedule" tab with 🔄 Start .

Monitoring the Load Process

Step 1

Now call the monitor with 🔲 . When you display the status, you see that your request has arrived in the persistent staging area (PSA) of the data retrieval area.

Monitor - Administrator Workbench

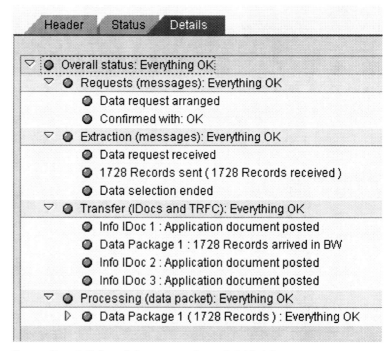

Figure: Monitoring – Requested Loaded to PSA © SAP AG

You can display the individual processing steps in the "Details" tab.

| Header | Status | Details |

▽ ● Overall status: Everything OK
　　▽ ● Requests (messages): Everything OK
　　　　● Data request arranged
　　　　● Confirmed with: OK
　　▽ ● Extraction (messages): Everything OK
　　　　● Data request received
　　　　● 1728 Records sent (1728 Records received)
　　　　● Data selection ended
　　▽ ● Transfer (IDocs and TRFC): Everything OK
　　　　● Info IDoc 1 : Application document posted
　　　　● Data Package 1 : 1728 Records arrived in BW
　　　　● Info IDoc 2 : Application document posted
　　　　● Info IDoc 3 : Application document posted
　　▽ ● Processing (data packet): Everything OK
　　　▷ ● Data Package 1 (1728 Records) : Everything OK

Figure: Details Tab with Processing Steps © SAP AG

Step 2

As a control, you can click ⊟ here to display the PSA directly. Of the loaded records, we will only display 10 in the following.

Selecting....	
...No. of Records	10
...From Record	
...From Segment	📄
All records	📄

✔ 📊 📊 🔻 ✖

Figure: Display Records in the PSA © SAP AG

Maintenance of PSA data request REQU_41KPY631CFHRXU)

🖉 ❖ 🖨 🔻 📊 📊 🔻 Σ 🔁 ℹ Data records to be edited

Status	DataPacket	Data rec.	Sales Offi	Product	Distributi	Calendar Y	Quantity	Base Unit	Revenue
○	1	1	1010	1	02	200301	11	PC	30789.0
○	1	2	1010	1	03	200301	12	PC	36946.8
○	1	3	1010	1	05	200301	15	PC	44504.1
○	1	4	1010	2	02	200301	18	PC	167022.
○	1	5	1010	2	03	200301	19	PC	193931.
○	1	6	1010	2	05	200301	13	PC	127864.
○	1	7	1010	3	02	200301	14	PC	110530.
○	1	8	1010	3	03	200301	12	PC	104214.
○	1	9	1010	3	05	200301	15	PC	125530.
○	1	10	1010	4	02	200301	14	PC	3066.00

Figure: PSA Data © SAP AG

Step 3

Click 🔙 to return to the monitor and update the data manually in the InfoCube.

Monitor - Administrator Workbench

Figure: Manual Data Update in the InfoCube © SAP AG

You then refresh the display with **All** as you can see in the status, the data has been updated successfully.

Figure: Monitor Status Display After Successful Update © SAP AG

Step 4

Click to exit the transaction.

Displaying Data in the InfoCube

First, we want to display the data directly in the InfoCube.

Step 1

Open the context menu of the InfoCube and choose Manage in order to verify
the data directly in the InfoCube.

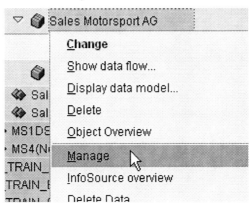

Figure: Administering the InfoCube © SAP AG

Step 2

The "Requests" shows the data package (request) that was just updated with the
status OOO.

Contents	Performance	Requests	Rollup	Collapse	Reconstruction

InfoCube requests for InfoCube:Sales Analysis Case Study(MB1DR01)										
Requ...	R...	C...	C...	R...	QM...	Te...	Dis...	InfoPackage	Request D...	Update
59565	▦				OOO	OOO	▦	Upload Sales Data	13.02.2006	13.02.:

Figure: Administering the Data Targets – Request © SAP AG

The ▦ symbol indicates that the request is available for reporting, which means
the data will be displayed in subsequent reports. If an error occurs, the data is

153

updated in the InfoCube (and can be examined and checked there), but has an inconsistent state and is therefore not displayed in reporting. In this case, the request status changes to

⬤⬤⬤ or ⬤⬤⬤ [.

Note

All further requests are set to status ⬤⬤⬤ and are not available for reporting until the incorrect data package has been checked and corrected (if necessary).

Step 3

You can display the InfoCube data directly in the "Content" tab, with InfoCube Content .

We can now restrict the selection. For example, we could restrict the values for the sales office or only select data from a certain interval. We will not do so here, however; instead, we press the "Field Selection for Output" button.

Data tgt. browser: 'MB1DR01', Selection scrn

| Fld Selectn for Output | Execute in Bckgrnd |

Product

Article		to	
Article(SID)		to	
Division[Article]		to	
Division[Article](SID)		to	

Sales

Distribution Channel		to	
Distribution Channel(SID)		to	
Sales Office		to	
Sales Office(SID)		to	
Company code[Sales O		to	
Company code[Sales O(SID)		to	
Country[Sales Office		to	
Country[Sales Office(SID)		to	

Figure: Selection Screen for InfoCube Data © SAP AG

Additional data selection parameters can be selected in the lower section of the screen. You will see that the number of hits is limited.

Note

Parameter Use DB Aggregation lets you aggregate (usually totaling) records. If this parameter is not set, the individual records will be displayed.

Figure: Parameterization of Selection © SAP AG

Note that only the values for the key figures in the InfoCube are displayed by default. Because we also care about the characteristic values, however, we select the following characteristics below. .

Figure: Choose Fields for Output © SAP AG

You start data selection with the ⊕ symbol and see the content of the InfoCube. You have a chance to verify all the values of the characteristics and key figures at this point.

Data tgt. browser: "MB1DR01", List output

Article	Division	0DISTR_CHA	Sales Office	0COMP_CODE	Country key	MB1DPRICU	MB1DQUAN	Discount	MB1DREVG	MB1DF
5	60	02	1010	9000	DE	0,00	0,000	1.005,40	7.960,00	6.95
6	60	02	1010	9000	DE	0,00	0,000	932,72	8.217,00	7.28
1	63	02	1010	9000	DE	2.799,00	15,000	3.306,19	41.985,00	38.67
2	61	02	1010	9000	DE	9.279,00	18,000	21.342,27	167.022,00	145.67
3	62	02	1010	9000	DE	7.895,00	13,000	12.152,36	102.635,00	90.48
4	60	02	1010	9000	DE	0,00	0,000	305,74	2.628,00	2.32
5	60	02	1010	9000	DE	0,00	0,000	391,97	3.582,00	3.19
6	60	02	1010	9000	DE	0,00	0,000	474,05	4.482,00	4.00
1	63	02	1010	9000	DE	2.799,00	13,000	3.276,27	36.387,00	33.11
2	61	02	1010	9000	DE	9.279,00	16,000	18.244,56	148.464,00	130.21

Figure: Output InfoCube Contents © SAP AG

Display Data Flow

Having reached the end of this section, now open the context menu for the InfoCube and choose "Display Data Flow" to show the entire data flow of the transaction data in a graphical overview.

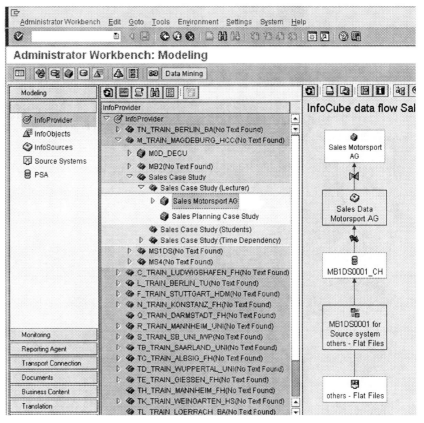

Figure: Display Overall Data Flow of Transaction Data © SAP AG

VI

From InfoCube to Data Analysis

This section describes the creation of a query from the InfoCube, as well as the available navigation options within a report.

SAP BI Business Explorer

The SAP BI Business Explorer (BEx) is the SAP Business Information Warehouse component that provides flexible reporting and analysis tools for strategic analyses and decision-making support within a company. These tools include query, reporting, and analysis functions. As an employee with access authorization, you can evaluate past or current data on various levels of detail and from different perspectives not only on the Web but also in Microsoft Excel.

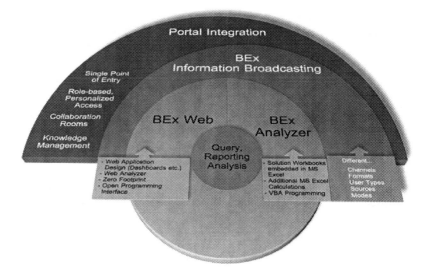

Figure: SAP BI Business Explorer © SAP AG

The Business Explorer consists of three components:

- The BEx Analyzer provides access to and analyses of data in SAP BW from within Microsoft Excel.

- BEx Web lets you use OLAP navigation in the Web and create management cockpits.

- BEx Information Broadcasting lets you distribute Business Intelligence content from SAP BW by e-mail either as precalculated documents with historical data, or as links with live data. You can also publish it to the Enterprise Portal.

Integration of the two areas is seamless: You can display queries from the BEx Analyzer with one click in a standard view in the Web browser. Likewise, you can also export a Web application to Microsoft Excel.

SAP BI Business Explorer Analyzer

A query is a question placed against the data structure of the InfoCube. The BEx Analyzer contains a number of tools that let users freely combine the InfoCube objects in a graphical user interface. The actual (technical) database access remains concealed from the user.

Calling the BEx Analyzer

The BEx Query Designer is a component of the BEx Analyzer.

Step 1

Start the BEx Analyzer from the Microsoft Windows Start menu, under entry Business Explorer.

You may see a security warning from Excel, stating that macros can contain viruses. Because you trust the source, activate the macros with

Figure: Starting the BEx Analyzer © SAP AG

The Microsoft Excel add-in for the SAP Business Explorer Analyzer appears.

Figure: BEx Analyzer Microsoft Excel Add-In (c) SAP AG

Note

The BEx Analyzer can also be started directly from the Administrator Workbench in SAP BW. To do so, start transaction rrmx in the SAP menu.
This is very practical for BW application developers; end users use the Microsoft Windows Start menu.

Step 2

You now select menu item Queries in the BEx Analyzer, as you want to create your first query. You then log on to the system.

Figure: Calling a Query © SAP AG

Selecting an InfoCube Step 3
for the Query

Now choose in the BEx Analyzer: Select Query "New".

Figure: Create a New Query © SAP AG

The Query Designer appears with an overview of all InfoAreas in which the InfoProviders that you are authorized to access are saved.

Step 4

Select the InfoCube [3] in the corresponding InfoArea [1]. Display the technical name of the InfoCubes, just to be sure [2]. Finally, click OK to confirm the selection [4].

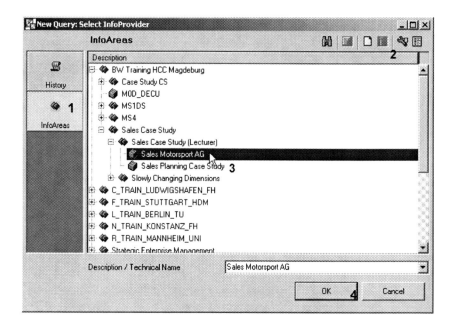

Figure: Selecting an InfoProvider © SAP AG

Our InfoCube, "Sales Motorsport AG", appears the Query Designer as follows. You can click the plus and minus signs to display the key figures and characteristics of the dimensions.

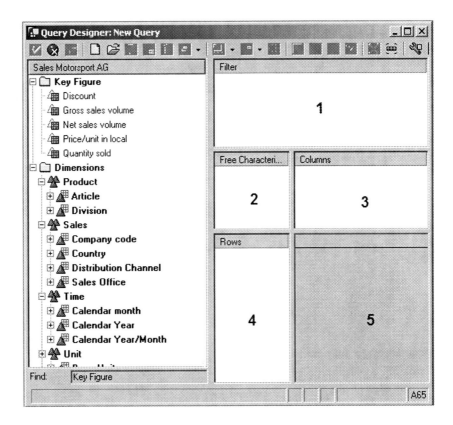

Figure: Query Designer © SAP AG

The right half of the Query Designer contains five areas. You copy the key figures and characteristics to the Rows [4] and Columns [3] areas via Drag&Drop; they will be displayed in this form later in the Excel workbook. Area [5] shows a preview. The "Free Characteristics" [2] area contains all the characteristics that will not be displayed immediately after the query is executed. These "free" characteristics can be used later for navigation. In the upper area, "Filters" [1], you can restrict certain areas – for example, you can restrict the Country to "Germany".

Functions of the BEx Query Designer

Before we continue with the query, we will first look at the following diagram to get an overview of the individual functions available in the BEx Query Designer. Some of these functions are examined more closely later in this section. Detailed descriptions of all functions are available in the online help.

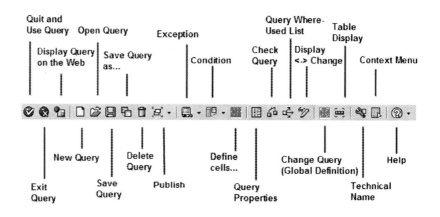

Figure: Functions of the BEx Query Designer © SAP AG

Creating Queries

We now ant to create our first query, and assume the following scenario:

Mr. Strong, Sales Manager in Germany, needs a list of the most successful sales offices from the year 2004. He wants the list to be arranged by country and sales office. He also wants to be able to break down the figures by article and division.

Creating Queries

We can now start building the report in the BEx Query Designer.

Step 1

We copy the key figures "Gross Sales Volume", "Discount", "Net Sales Volume" and "Quantity Sold" to the columns and characteristics "Country" and "Sales Office" to the rows.

Step 2

In addition, select the characteristics Division and Article as "free characteristics", which we will use for navigation later in the Excel workbook.

Step 3

We also use a filter to restrict the calendar year to the values from 2004. To do so, we drag the "Calendar Year" characteristic to the Filters area, where we open the context menu (right mouse button) and select Restrict. Select the fixed value "2004" and click OK to confirm.

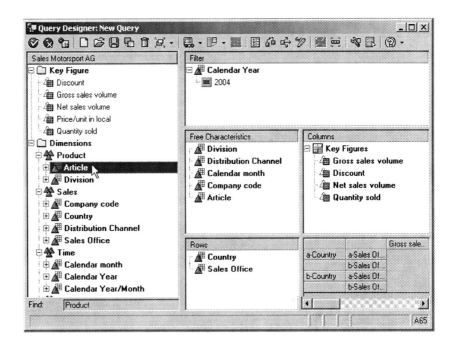

Figure: Creating a New Query © SAP AG

Saving Queries

Step 4

Save the query 💾, assign the technical name MB1D001 and the description "Sales Volume by Country and Sales Office".

Executing a Query

Step 5

You now execute the query with 🕢 and see the result embedded in an Excel workbook.

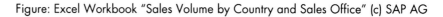
Division					
Distribution Channel					
Calendar month					
Company code					
Article					
Key Figures					
Country					
Sales Office					
Calendar Year		2004			
Country		Sales Office		Gross sales volume	Discount	Ne
Switzerland		9200	Montreux	57.140.842,13 CHF	4.108.116,53 CHF	53.
		Result		57.140.842,13 CHF	4.108.116,53 CHF	53.
Germany		1010	Hamburg	38.012.335,33 EUR	2.880.835,38 EUR	35.
		9000	Magdeburg	29.087.614,98 EUR	2.167.742,85 EUR	26.
		9100	München	44.229.008,25 EUR	3.177.454,31 EUR	41.
		Result		111.328.958,56 EUR	8.226.032,54 EUR	103.
Overall Result				168.469.800,69 MIX	12.334.149,07 MIX	156

Figure: Excel Workbook "Sales Volume by Country and Sales Office" (c) SAP AG

Step 6

You can see that the column width for the country has been sized to fit the header for the workbook. You can change these properties with menu item "OLAP Functions for Active Cell".

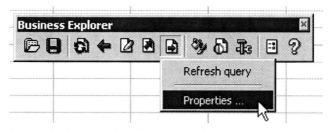

Figure: Calling Workbook Properties © SAP AG

Step 7

You can configure the properties in the "Column Width" tab page such that the cells are resized for the new values automatically after a data refresh. To do so, choose radio button "Adjust to results area"

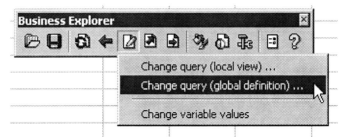

Figure: Adapt Column Width to Result Area © SAP AG

When you refresh the query with ![icon] you see that the width of the first column was adapted to the results area. You can also see that the query results contain different currencies. This is indicated by the MIX entry in the cells, which we will describe in more detail later.

Changing Queries

The requirements of queries often change over time. The queries then have to be modified in order to meet the new requirements.

Changing Queries Directly

You can change the definition of a query directly from within a report in the BEx Analyzer.

Figure: Change Query from Within Workbook © SAP AG

Two options are available:

1. Change Query (Local View): You can change the arrangement of key figures and characteristics in the lines and columns of the current workbook regardless of your authorizations.

2. Change Query (Global Definition): This changes the definition of the query in all workbooks. Therefore, the changes affect all objects that use the query. Specific authorization is required for such changes.

Choose **Change Query (Global Definition)** and the BEx Query Designer appears again.

Aside: Finding a Query

Queries can be changed directly after you log on to the BEx Analyzer. But how can you find a defined query?

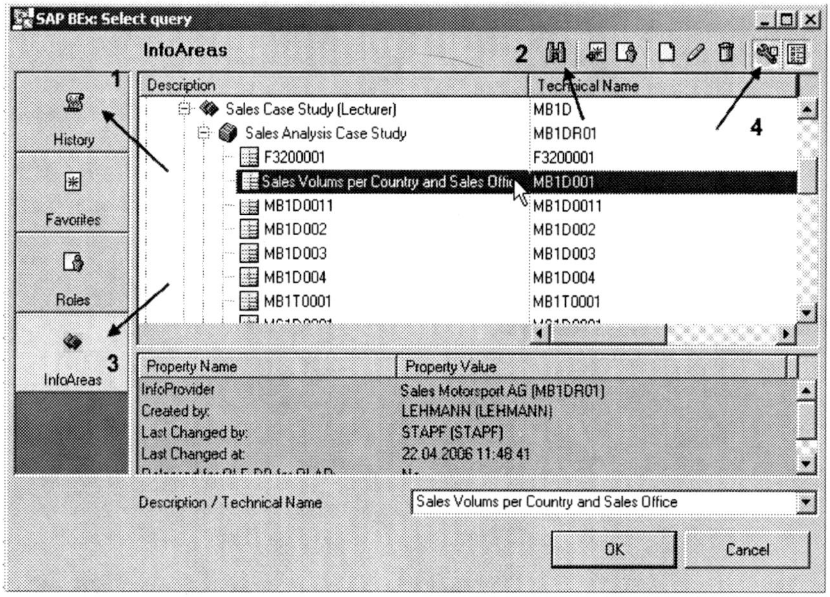

Figure: Select Query © SAP AG

Option 1

Select the query you want to change in the initial menu, "SAP BEx: Select Query". You can find the desired query in the history [1]. The most recently created queries are displayed here chronologically.

Option 2

You can use the search [2] to find queries by technical name or description.

Option 3

You can also find the query in the InfoArea [3] section, beneath the specific

InfoProvider for which it was defined. In our case, the query was defined for InfoCube "Sales Motorsport AG" and can therefore be found there.

These two buttons ![buttons] let you display the technical names and properties in addition to the descriptions, as shown in the diagram [4].

Changing Object Properties

A query is built from key figures and characteristics. A wide variety of formatting options is available for displaying these objects in report. The default properties for displaying the values in the Business Explorer are defined when an InfoObject is created; end users can change them during query definition.

Properties of
Characteristics

You can define properties for the individual characteristics through their context menus.

We now want to change the display attributes of the Sales Office characteristic. We don't like the fact that both the key and the texts appear in the report.

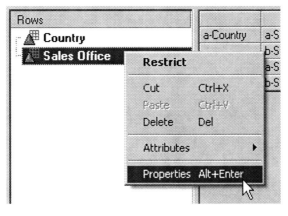

Figure: Changing Characteristic Properties 1 © SAP AG

Figure: Changing Characteristic Properties 2 © SAP AG

Option 1

Display as [1]: You can define how the individual characteristic values are displayed here. You can choose between "Text", "Key", and "Key and Text".

Step 1

Display the Sales Office characteristic as Text.

Option 2

[2] Display of Results: This function lets you change the appearance of the characteristics in the reports. Firstly, you can choose whether to display the results rows Never, Always or Only for One Value. Under Normalize to , key figures are displayed as a percentage of the selected result, which can be the query result, a partial result, or the overall result.

Step 2

Save the following settings:

- Suppress Results Rows: Never

- Normalize to: No Normalization

Option 3

[3] Sort Order: You can also define a sort sequence within the characteristic. You can sort by text or key in ascending or descending order.

Step 3

Choose sort sequence **Sales Office by Text Ascending** and display the **Country characteristic as Text.**

Properties of Key Figures

You can also configure the properties of key figures through their context menus (see next diagram).

[1] Display: You can highlight the display of a key figure in a report. You can also suppress key figures that are only required for calculations, to prevent them from appearing in the report.

[2] Number format: You can define a scaling factor to the key figure, determine the number of decimal places, and/or select plus/minus sign reversal.

[3] Calculations: This function lets you recalculate results or single values according to specific criteria.

[4] Currency translation: You can define a translation type or configure a target currency in this area.

Step 5

To better compare the sales of the German and Swiss sales offices, we define currency translation type TO_EURO for Gross Sales Volume.

Figure: Properties of Key Figures © SAP AG

Step 6

Save the query and execute it again .

Step 7

You can use menu path Layout -> Display Text Elements -> All in the Business Explorers menu to display information about the author, InfoProviders, data status, and so on.

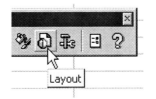

Figure: Changing the Report Layout © SAP AG

Once you configure all of the above settings, our workbook now looks like this:

Sales Volume by Country and Sales Office

Division	
Distribution Channel	
Calendar month	
Company code	
Article	
Key Figures	
Country	
Sales Office	

| Calendar Year | 2004 |

Author	LEHMANN
Last Changed by	STAPF
InfoProvider	MB1DR01
Query Technical Name	MB1D001
Key Date	28.08.2006
Changed At	28.08.2006 09:26:15
Status of Data	13.02.2006 18:55:34
Current User	STAPF
Last Refreshed	28.08.2006 09:55:38

Country	Sales Office	Gross sales volume	Discount	Net sales volume	Quantity sold
Switzerland	Montreux	57.140.842,13 CHF	4.108.116,53 CHF	53.032.725,60 CHF	4.591 PC
	Result	57.140.842,13 CHF	4.108.116,53 CHF	53.032.725,60 CHF	4.591 PC
Germany	Hamburg	38.012.335,33 EUR	2.880.835,38 EUR	35.131.499,95 EUR	5.013 PC
	Magdeburg	29.087.614,98 EUR	2.167.742,85 EUR	26.919.872,13 EUR	3.895 PC
	München	44.229.008,25 EUR	3.177.454,31 EUR	41.051.553,94 EUR	5.872 PC
	Result	111.328.958,56 EUR	8.226.032,54 EUR	103.102.926,02 EUR	14.780 PC
Overall Result		168.469.800,69 MIX	12.334.149,07 MIX	156.135.651,62 MIX	19.371 PC

Figure: Workbook After Update © SAP AG

Navigating in the Query

The context menu features various navigation options within the report output. Several other functions are also available, depending on the cell context, and are described in further detail below.

Filtering Values

In this section, we are only interested in the values from the German sales offices.

Step 1

You can select a filter value directly in the results area of an executed report. To do so, position the cursor on the filter value (Germany in this example), open the context menu, and choose "Keep Filter Value...".

Calendar Year	2004	
Country	Sales Office	Gross sales volum·
Switzerland	Montreux	37.141.547,38 EU
	Result	37.141.547,38 EU
Germany		.335,33 EU
	Back to Start	.614,98 EU
	Keep Filter Value	.008,25 EU
	Filter and drilldown according to ▶	.958,56 EU

Figure: Keep Filter Value © SAP AG

As you can see, the selected value is displayed in the filter cells above the query results area [2]. The calendar year was already selected during query definition, and also appears in the filter cells [1].

	A	B	C
	Sales Volume by Country and Sales Offi		
	Calendar Year/Month		
	Article		
	Company code		
	Distribution Channel		
	Division		
	Key figures		
	Country	Germany	
]	Sales Office		
1			
2	Calendar Year	2004	
3			
4	Sales Office	Gross sales volume	Net sales volume
5	Hamburg	38.012.335,33 EUR	35.131.499,95 EUR
5	Magdeburg	29.087.614,98 EUR	26.919.872,13 EUR
7	München	44.229.008,25 EUR	41.051.553,94 EUR
3	Overall Result	111.328.958,56 EUR	103.102.926,02 EUR

Figure: Selected Values © SAP AG

Note

You can also select values from the context menu of the characteristics in the filter cells

Insert Drilldown According to

Step 2

In order to enable comparison of the individual articles in the various sales offices, we add a drilldown according to Articles to the sales offices.

Sales Office	Gross sales volume	Net sales volume	Discount
Hamburg		5.131.499,95 EUR	2.880.835,38 EUR
Magdeburg		6.919.872,13 EUR	2.167.742,85 EUR
München		1.051.553,94 EUR	3.177.454,31 EUR
Overall Resul		3.102.926,02 EUR	8.226.032,54 EUR

Context menu overlay:
- Back
- Back to Start
- Keep Filter Value
- Filter and drilldown according to ▶
- Add Drilldown According to ▶
  - Calendar Year/Month
  - Company code
  - Country
  - Distribution Channel
  - Division
  - **Article**
- Swap Sales Office with ▶
- Sort ▶
- Goto ▶
- Currency Translation ▶

Figure: Filter and Drilldown According to Article © SAP AG

Step 3

Now display the results rows of all characteristics again. The report now looks like this diagram.

Sales Volume by Country and Sales Office

Calendar Year/Month	
Article	
Company code	
Distribution Channel	
Division	
Key figures	
Country	Germany
Sales Office	

Calendar Year	2004

Sales Office	Article	Gross sales volume	Net sales volume	Discount
Hamburg	Scooter 125	4.928.606,60 EUR	4.544.109,36 EUR	384.497,24
	Cruise 750	17.385.119,58 EUR	16.060.066,02 EUR	1.325.053,56
	Motocross 800	14.458.832,80 EUR	13.376.156,95 EUR	1.082.675,85
	Leather Jacket	412.122,32 EUR	382.270,37 EUR	29.851,95
	Helmet K4 black	359.890,93 EUR	335.611,75 EUR	24.279,18
	Inspection	467.763,10 EUR	433.285,50 EUR	34.477,60
	Result	38.012.335,33 EUR	35.131.499,95 EUR	2.880.835,38
Magdeburg	Scooter 125	4.036.283,42 EUR	3.736.781,17 EUR	299.502,25
	Cruise 750	13.621.019,91 EUR	12.621.076,02 EUR	999.943,89
	Motocross 800	10.486.915,14 EUR	9.685.161,82 EUR	801.753,32
	Leather Jacket	298.925,84 EUR	278.540,14 EUR	20.385,70
	Helmet K4 black	296.787,37 EUR	275.743,06 EUR	21.044,31
	Inspection	347.683,30 EUR	322.569,92 EUR	25.113,38
	Result	29.087.614,98 EUR	26.919.872,13 EUR	2.167.742,85
München	Scooter 125	5.894.860,29 EUR	5.465.605,83 EUR	429.254,46
	Cruise 750	19.675.617,52 EUR	18.265.375,14 EUR	1.410.242,38
	Motocross 800	17.206.522,54 EUR	15.972.438,35 EUR	1.234.084,19
	Leather Jacket	479.795,44 EUR	446.345,28 EUR	33.450,16
	Helmet K4 black	421.470,34 EUR	390.103,83 EUR	31.366,51
	Inspection	550.742,12 EUR	511.685,51 EUR	39.056,61
	Result	44.229.008,25 EUR	41.051.553,94 EUR	3.177.454,31
Overall Result		111.328.958,56 EUR	103.102.926,02 EUR	8.226.032,54

Figure: Query After Various Navigation Steps © SAP AG

Translating Currencies

You notice that the net sales volume and discount are displayed in different currencies, and want to standardize the display.

Step 1

Open the context menu of a key figure and choose "Currency Translation" and then By Target Currency from Database Currency".

	Net sales volume	Discount	Quantity
8 EUR	53.032.725,60 CHF	4.199.116,63 CHF	4.591 PC
8 EUR	53.032.725,60 C	Back to Start	4.591 PC
3 EUR	35.131.499,95 E		5.013 PC
8 EUR	26.919.872,13 E	Sort ▶	3.895 PC
5 EUR	41.051.553,94 E	Calculate ▶	5.872 PC
6 EUR	103.102.926,02 E		4.780 PC
4 EUR	156.135.651,62	Goto ▶	9.371 PC
		Currency Translation ▶	By Target Currency from Database Currency
		All Characteristics ▶	By Target Currency Using Definition Currency
			By Database Currency
		Properties ...	✓ As Defined in Query

Figure: Currency Translation © SAP AG

Step 2

You can now enter a target currency, such as USD, and define a translation type. The exchange rate is automatically created using the selected translation type.

You want all the values to appear in euros.

☞ Currency Translation

Targ.Curr. [   ]

Conversion Type TO_EURO ⬚

⊕ ⬚ ✖

Figure: Currency Translation to EUR ©

Translation type TO_EURO does not require the specification of a target currency; in fact, if a target currency is specified, an error message will result.

Attaching a Chart

You now want to attach a diagram to the query results.

Step 1

To do so, you first swap the Country and Sales Office characteristics.

Country	Sales Office	Gross sales volume	Net sales volur
Switzerland	Montroux	27.141.547,38 EUR	34.471.271,64
		47,38 EUR	34.471.271,64
Germany		35,33 EUR	35.131.499,95
		4,98 EUR	26.919.872,13
		08,25 EUR	41.051.553,94
		58,56 EUR	103.102.926,02
Overall Result		05,94 EUR	137.574.197,66

Context menu:
- Back
- Back to Start
- Keep Filter Value
- Filter and drilldown according to ▶
- Add Drilldown According to ▶
- **Swap Country with** ▶
  - Calendar Year/Month
  - Company code
  - Distribution Channel
  - Division
  - Product
  - **Sales Office**
  - Structure
- Sort ▶
- Goto ▶
- Currency Translation ▶
- Country ▶

Figure: Swap Characteristics © SAP AG

Step 2

Now suppress the yellow results rows for all the characteristics, so they do not appear in the chart.

nd		Montreux	37.141.547,38 EUR	34.471.271,64 EUR	2.670.275,74 EUR

The context menu overlays the table. Menu items:

- Back — | 47,38 EUR | 34.471.271,64 EUR | 2.670.275,74 EUR |
- Back to Start — | 35,33 EUR | 35.131.499,95 EUR | 2.880.835,38 EUR |
- Keep Filter Value — | 14,98 EUR | 26.919.872,13 EUR | 2.167.742,85 EUR |
- Filter and drilldown according to ▶ — | 08,25 EUR | 41.051.553,94 EUR | 3.177.454,31 EUR |
- Add Drilldown According to ▶ — | 58,56 EUR | 103.102.926,02 EUR | 8.226.032,54 EUR |
- Swap Country with ▶ — | 05,94 EUR | 137.574.197,66 EUR | 10.896.308,28 EUR |
- Sort ▶
- Goto ▶
- Currency Translation ▶
- Country ▶
- All Characteristics ▶
  - Display as ▶
  - Position of Results Rows ▶
  - Suppress Results Rows ▶
    - ✓ Never
    - Always
    - Conditional
  - Suppress Zero Columns/Rows
  - Normalize ▶
  - Undo ▶
- Properties ...

Figure: Suppress Results Rows

Step 3

Now use menu item "Layout" in the Business Explorers to attach a chart.

Business Explorer

- Attach chart
- Attach map

Figure: Attaching a Chart © SAP AG

The chart adjusts itself automatically to any updates in the data constellation. A new sales office, for example, would appear in the display immediately.

Figure: Attaching a Chart © SAP AG

From Query to Management Cockpit

This section describes the setup of a Management Cockpit.

We will first create two queries and then use them to build a Management Cockpit. Like in the previous chapter, we will use the SAP BEx Analyzer to create the queries, which will then serve as data providers for the cockpit.

We will use the SAP BEx Web Application Designer to create the cockpit itself. The Designer is located in the same Windows program group as the SAP BEx Analyzer.

We want our Management Cockpit to display the sales volumes from 2004, broken down by division, as well as an overview of the sales volumes by month in the same year. To do so, we first create the two queries: "Cockpit: Sales Volume by Division" und "Cockpit: Sales Volume by Month". The InfoProvider is InfoCube "Sales Motorsport AG" in both cases.

Sales Volume by Division

We will first create a query that displays the sales volumes by division.

Step 1

Make the following selection in BEx Query Designer:

- Characteristic "Division" in the rows
- Key figures "Gross Sales Volume" and "Net Sales Volume" in the columns

183

- The article as a free characteristic

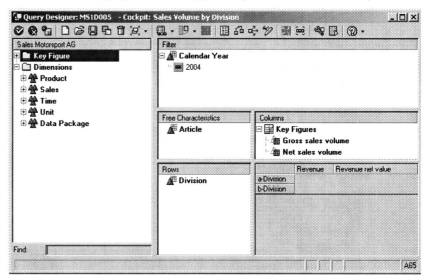

Step 2

Because we are only interested in the values from 2004, set the filter accordingly.

Step 3

We want to display all the values in "Euros", and therefore have the system translate the two key figures accordingly through context menu item Properties.

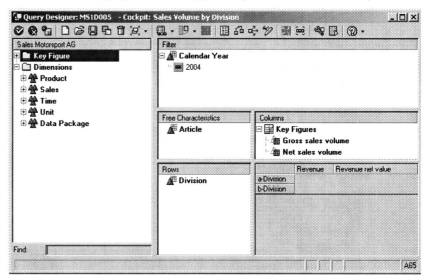

Figure: Query Design "Sales Volume by Division" © SAP AG

Finally, save the query as "Cockpit: Sales Volume by Division" and execute it.

Sales Volume by Month

We will now create a query to serve as the second data supplier for the cockpit. Proceed analogous to the first query above:

Step 1

Make the following selection in BEx Query Designer:

- Characteristic "Calendar Year/Month" in the rows

- Key figures "Gross Sales Volume" and "Net Sales Volume" in the columns

Step 2

Again, because we are only interested in the values from 2004, set the filter accordingly.

Figure: Query Design "Sales Volume by Month" © SAP AG

Translate the values from the gross and net sales volumes into euros again. Save the query as "Cockpit: Sales Volume by Month" and execute it.

Web Application Designer

The data providers have been defined, and we can now begin building the cockpit. To do so, start the SAP BEx Web Application Designer from the Windows Start menu. After logon, the Design Editor appears.

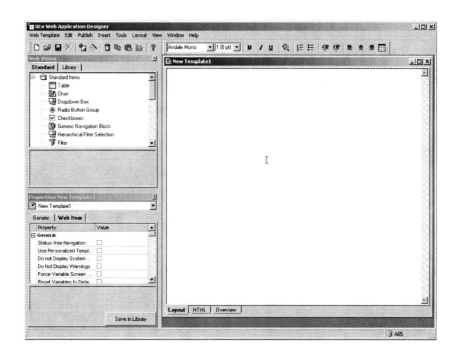

Figure: BEx Web Application Designer © SAP AG

Define Rough Layout

We first define a rough layout.

Step 1

To start, create a header or chart in the layout window, along with a table with Insert – Table. The table is supposed to have two rows and two columns.

Step 2

You then use the Web items "Table" and "Chart" to fill the table cells. These objects appear in the "Web – Items" area, where you can drag and drop them to the layout (you may need some practice before you master this technique completely).

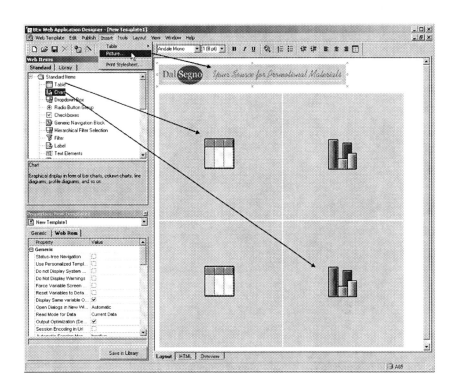

Figure: Copying Web Items to the Layout © SAP AG

The next step is to define the properties for the objects in the individual cells.

Defining Object Properties

We now want to arrange the tables and the charts in order to fit them on a page.

Step 1

Define the properties for Table 1.

- Name: Dataprovider_1
- Query: "Cockpit: Sales Volume by Division"
- Border Type: With Border

Properties: New Template1 ✕

TABLE_1 ▼

Generic | Web Item

Name	TABLE_1
Master Web Item	ble (CL_RSR_WWW_ITEM_GRID)

DataProvider
Name	DATAPROVIDER_1 ▼
Query / View	Cockpit: Revenue by Division (

Figure: Define General Properties of a Table © SAP AG

Step 2

Define the properties for Chart 1.

- Name: Dataprovider_1
- Query: "Cockpit: Sales Volume by Division"
- Border Type: With Border
- Width in pixels: 550
- Height in pixels: 200
- Swap display axes
- Automatic display of units and currencies

Properties: New Template1		✕
🔳 CHART_1		▼

Generic | **Web Item**

Property	Value	▲
Width in Pixels ➝	550	
Height ➝	200	
Border Type ➝	With Border	
Collapsed	☐	
Hide Object	☐	
Objects with Navigation ...	☑	
⊟ **Specific**		
Edit Chart	Columns	
Suppress Sums	☑	
Swap Display Axes	☑ ⬅	
Hide Expanded Hierarch...	☐	
Data Providers Affected	(List)	
Automatic Display of Uni...	☑	
Chart Title (Language D...		
Chart Subtitle (Languag...		
Category Axis (X): Title		▼

Figure: Define Properties for Chart 1 © SAP AG

Step 3

You want to use the query "Cockpit: Sales Volume by Month" as the data provider for Table 2. Therefore, you first have to create a new data provider for this Web item with 🔲 [1] and then assign the query to this data provider (Dataprovider_2).

Figure: Create New Data Provider and Assign it to Query © SAP AG

Step 4

Assign the following properties to Chart 2:

- Name: Dataprovider_2
- Query: "Cockpit: Sales Volume by Month"
- Border Type: With Border
- Width in pixels: 550
- Height in pixels: 300
- Swap display axes
- Automatic display of units and currencies

Figure: Define Properties of Web Item Chart © SAP AG

Once you have configured all the settings, save the draft in your favorites and

start the cockpit in the browser for the first time: .

Displaying the Cockpit   The Management Cockpit looks something like this in the browser:

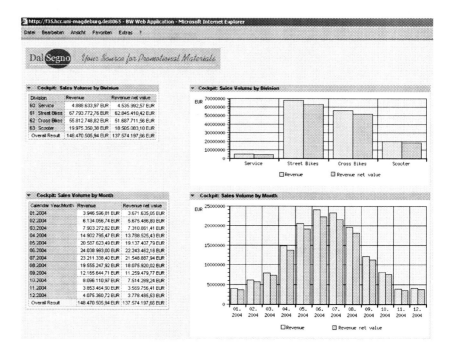

Figure: Management Cockpit in the Browser © SAP AG

Changing Charts

The chart that shows sales volumes by month clearly illustrates the seasonal sales curve. Sales in the winter months are much lower than those in summer. The display options are nearly limitless. By modifying the chart properties, you can – among other things – change the chart type. You could change it from a vertical bar chart to a line chart, for example.

Change the Web item of the lower chart to "Lines" and display the result.

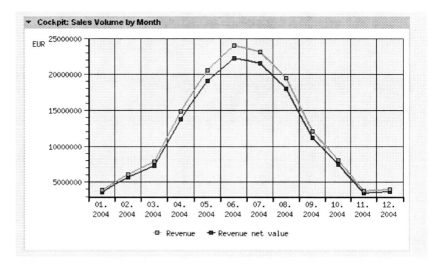

Figure: Sales Statistics as Line Chart © SAP AG

Navigation in the Web

There are also many options for navigating through the report in the Management Cockpit.

In this example, we want to display the articles from the division and sort the gross sales volumes to create a ranking of the months with the highest sales.

These functions are located in the context menus of characteristics "Division" and "Gross Sales Volume" respectively.

Figure: Add Drilldown © SAP AG

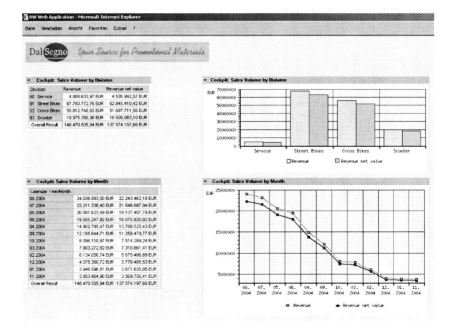

Figure: Web Report After Further Navigation Steps © SAP AG

VII

Slowly Changing Dimensions

The modeling of multi-dimensional structures is often dependent on business requirements that change frequently over time. The version management of master data plays an important role here. In addition to the current display of attributes, the display of the history – referred to as slowly changing dimensions – plays a major role. When a salesperson moves to a different sales office, for example, this change is usually not supposed to affect the data from before the change, and the old entries in the database table cannot simply be overwritten. The slowly changing dimensions represent a concept for avoiding such conflicts. In addition, the key date-related display is part of the daily routine for a data warehouse. The three different modeling methods are described below, based on an example.

Introductory Example

A salesperson always works in a specific sales office. However, the sales person can move over time.

Scenario

Salesperson Mr. Huber worked in sales office 9000 (Magdeburg) until February

28, 2005. He moved to sales office 9200 (Montreux) on March 1, 2005.

In the first example, we deal with the interesting issue of what happens to the salesperson's sales when he moves to a new sales office. Management requirements are twofold in this context.

Current Display
- The decisive factor in the current display is which sales office the salesperson worked in at the time the query is executed. Therefore, the query is supposed to display all the salesperson's sales in the new sales office, although past sales were made in a different office.

Time Dependency
- In the time-dependent case, a key date is defined, and the report is supposed to work with the sales office that was valid on that key date. This makes it possible, for example, to determine how the sales of a sales office would have been if the salesperson had not moved.

Historical Truth
- Considering the historical truth, the decisive factor is which sales office the salesperson belonged to at the time of its sales process. Consequently, the sales made in past periods stay with the according sales office.

Implementation with SAP BW

We will now work through the above statements based on example. To do so, we first add a new InfoObject, Salesperson, to our case study.

Creating InfoObjects

Step 1

We first create an InfoObject called "Salesperson". To do so, enter technical name MB1DVEND and configure the following parameters:

- General tab: Data Type CHAR, 20-character
- Business Explorer tab: Display as key in the Business Explorer
- Master Data tab: with master data, without texts

- Attributes tab: sales office MB1DSALOF as a navigation attribute, description: "Sales Office (Attribute of Salesperson)".

- Attribute tab: The sales office is time-dependent!

Business Explorer	○ Master data/texts	Hierarchy	○ Attributes	Compo..

| | | | | | Navigation Attribute InfoProvider | |

Attributes: Detail/Navigation Attributes

Attribute	Long description	Typ	Time-Dependent	O...	N...	T...	Navigation att. des
MB1DSALOF	Sales Office	NAV	☑	0		☐	Sales Office (Attribu
				0		☐	

Figure: Time Dependency © SAP AG

Entering the Master Data

Generate the InfoObject and then enter the following master data manually:

Salesperson	Valid from	Valid to	Sales Office
BAUER	01/01/1000	12/31/9999	9000
HUBER	01/01/1000	02/28/2005	9000
HUBER	03/01/2005	12/31/9999	9200
MÜLLER	01/01/1000	12/31/9999	1010
SCHMIDT	01/01/1000	12/31/9999	1010
SCHULZE	01/01/1000	12/31/9999	9200
MAIER	01/01/1000	12/31/9999	9200

Figure: Master Data – Salesperson © SAP AG

Creating InfoCube

Step 2

Now create a simple InfoCube with type **BasicCube**, technical name **MB1SC01**, and the description **Slowly Changing Dimensions**.

Figure: Create InfoCube © SAP AG

Defining the Structure

Select the **Salesperson (MB1DVEND)** as a characteristic. Also add the time characteristic **Calendar Year/Month (0CALMONTH)** and key figure **Gross Sales Volume (MB1DREVG)** to the InfoCube. Define the **Sales Office** (as Master Data Attribute) as a navigation attribute.

Figure: Define InfoCube © SAP AG

First define dimension Salesperson and then the Salesperson characteristic to it.

Figure: Assign Dimensions © SAP AG

Then generate the structure of the InfoCube, which now has the following simple structure:

Creating InfoSources

Step 3

Now create an InfoSource with MB1SC001 and flexible update for the sales data, and assign a PC_FILE as the source system.

Figure: Create InfoSource © SAP AG

Transfer Structure

Step 4

In the next step, add the following InfoObjects

- MB1DVEND (Salesperson)
- 0CALMONTH (Calendar Year/Month)
- MB1DREVG (Gross Sales Volume)
- 0CURRENCY (Currency)

to the transfer structure of the DataSource.

Figure: Define Transfer Structure © SAP AG

Transfer Rules

Step 5

You now generate the communication structure of the InfoSource and generate the transfer rules.

Figure: Define InfoSource © SAP AG

Defining Update Rules

Step 6

Before we begin loading the transaction data, we first have to define the update rules for the InfoCube. To do so, select InfoSource MB1SC001 as the data source and let SAP BW create the update rules.

Update Rules create: Start

InfoCube   MB1SC01   Slowly Changing Dimensions

Data Source
- ⦿ InfoSource   MB1SC001
- ○ ODS object
- ○ InfoCube

Figure: Create Update Rules © SAP AG

Then activate the InfoCube .

Loading Data

Step 7

Now load the data from the csv file to the InfoCube. To do so, create an InfoPackage for the DataSource and load the data directly into the InfoCube.

Slowly-Changing-Dimensions-LEH.csv – Editor

Datei Bearbeiten Format Ansicht ?

```
Sales person;Quarter;Revenue;Currency
BAUER;012005;100000;EUR
HUBER;012005;200000;EUR
MAIER;022005;150000;EUR
MÜLLER;012005;120000;EUR
SCHMIDT;012005;80000;EUR
SCHULZE;012005;140000;EUR
HUBER;022005;100000;EUR
BAUER;032005;100000;EUR
HUBER;032005;300000;EUR
MAIER;032005;200000;EUR
MÜLLER;032005;100000;EUR
SCHMIDT;032005;100000;EUR
SCHULZE;032005;110000;EUR
```

Figure: Transaction Data with Sales Volumes from Quarters 1-3.

Step 8

Check the data load process in the monitor or administration function for the InfoCube (see diagram below).

| Contents | Performance | Requests | Rollup | Collapse | Reconstruction |

InfoCube requests for InfoCube:Slowly Changing Dimensions(MB1SC01)

Requ...	R...	C...	C...	R...	QM...	Te...	Dis...	Transf...	Added ...	Type of Data Update	Info
57525					∞∞∞	∞∞∞	⊠	13	13	Full update	MB1:

Figure: Checking the Load Process © SAP AG

Defining Queries

Step 1

Define the following query.

Figure: Define Query © SAP AG

Current Display

Step 2

Save the query, then execute it with the following result. Sales by salesperson HUBER from the months January-March are assigned to sales office 9200 (Montreux), although he worked at sales office 9000 (Magdeburg) during this time. This represents the current display.

	A	B	C	D	E
1	Query for SCD				
2					
3	Structure				
4	Sales Office				
5	Sales person				
6	Calendar Year/Month				
7					
8	Sales Office (Attribut of Salesperson)		Sales person	Calendar Year/Month	Gross sales volume
9	1010	Hamburg	MÜLLER	01.2005	120.000,00 EUR
10				03.2005	100.000,00 EUR
11				Result	220.000,00 EUR
12			SCHMIDT	01.2005	80.000,00 EUR
13				03.2005	100.000,00 EUR
14				Result	180.000,00 EUR
15			Result		400.000,00 EUR
16	9000	Magdeburg	BAUER	01.2005	100.000,00 EUR
17				03.2005	100.000,00 EUR
18				Result	200.000,00 EUR
19			Result		200.000,00 EUR
20	9200	Montreux	HUBER	01.2005	200.000,00 EUR
21				02.2005	100.000,00 EUR
22				03.2005	300.000,00 EUR
23				Result	600.000,00 EUR
24			MAIER	02.2005	150.000,00 EUR
25				03.2005	200.000,00 EUR
26				Result	350.000,00 EUR
27			SCHULZE	01.2005	140.000,00 EUR
28				03.2005	110.000,00 EUR
29				Result	250.000,00 EUR
30			Result		1.200.000,00 EUR
31	Overall Result				1.800.000,00 EUR

Figure: Execute Query © SAP AG

Time Dependency

You can also valuate the sales volumes for a specific key date. To do so, enter a certain date (such as February 10, 2005) as the key date in the query properties.

Figure: Define Key Date-Related View

Now execute the query. You will see that the sales by salesperson HUBER are now allocated to sales office 9000 (Magdeburg), where he worked on the defined key date.

	A	B	C	D	E
1	Query for SCD				
2					
3	Structure				
4	Sales Office (Attribut of Salesperson)				
5	Sales person				
6	Calendar Year/Month				
7					
8	Sales Office (Attribut of Salesperson)		Sales person	Calendar Year/Month	Gross sales volume
9	1010	Hamburg	MÜLLER	01.2005	120.000,00 EUR
10				03.2005	100.000,00 EUR
11				Result	220.000,00 EUR
12			SCHMIDT	01.2005	80.000,00 EUR
13				03.2005	100.000,00 EUR
14				Result	180.000,00 EUR
15			Result		400.000,00 EUR
16	9000	Magdeburg	BAUER	01.2005	100.000,00 EUR
17				03.2005	100.000,00 EUR
18				Result	200.000,00 EUR
19			HUBER	01.2005	200.000,00 EUR
20				02.2005	100.000,00 EUR
21				03.2005	300.000,00 EUR
22				Result	600.000,00 EUR
23			Result		800.000,00 EUR
24	9200	Montreux	MAIER	02.2005	150.000,00 EUR
25				03.2005	200.000,00 EUR
26				Result	350.000,00 EUR
27			SCHULZE	01.2005	140.000,00 EUR
28				03.2005	110.000,00 EUR
29				Result	250.000,00 EUR
30			Result		600.000,00 EUR
31	Overall Result				1.800.000,00 EUR

Figure: Execute Query: Key Date-Specific View © SAP AG

In contrast, if you selected March 10, 2005 as the key date, Mr. Huber's total sales volume would be allocated to sales office 9200 (Montreux).

Historical Truth

We will now examine the implementation of the historical truth. In this approach, HUBER's sales from January and February should be allocated to sales office 9000 (Magdeburg), while sales from March should be allocated to sales office 9200 (Montreux).

We use a trick for this implementation, to improve performance: When data is loaded, the respective "Salesperson to Sales Office" assignment is read from the salesperson's master data for every transaction data record, and saved persistently in an additional InfoObject in the InfoCube.

This means we have to add characteristic MB1DSALOF "Sales Office" to our InfoCube. As a result, two "Sales Office" characteristics will appear later in the

Business Explorer:

1. Sales Office (attribute of salesperson)

2. Sales Office (characteristic in the InfoCube)

Step 1

You first have to add InfoObject Salesperson to the InfoCube, assign it to dimension "Salesperson", and generate.

Figure: Copying the Sales Office to the InfoCube © SAP AG

The InfoCube now looks like this for end users:

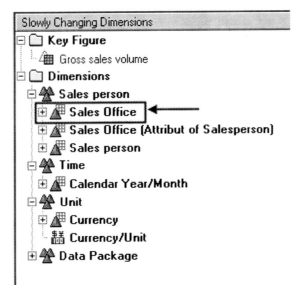

Figure: InfoCube with Sales Office © SAP AG

Update the InfoCube

The update of the InfoCube changes to inactive, because its structure has been changed.

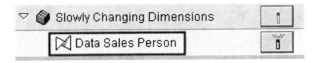

Figure: Inactive Update © SAP AG

Step 2

Change the update. You first have to make sure that the new "Sales Office" InfoObject in the InfoCube re-reads the respective value from the master data. This "re-reading" uses a method that determines the value from the salesperson's master data attribute and saves it persistently in the InfoObject of the InfoCube. The time dependency is defined through the reference to calendar year/month.

Figure: Generate Method for Sales Office Characteristic (in the InfoCube) © SAP AG

Figure: Define Time Dependency © SAP AG

Deleting Data in the Cube

Step 3

We now generate the InfoCube, and then delete the data from it. To do so, we choose "Manage" from the context menu of the InfoCube, select the loaded request, and start the delete program.

Figure: Deleting Data from the InfoCube © SAP AG

Reloading Data

Step 4

Now load the data from the PSA to the InfoCube again. The new update rules are used in the process, which means the salesperson's assignment to the sales office is read from the salesperson's master data.

Figure: Restructuring the InfoCube © SAP AG

Creating Queries

Now make a minor change to the query: Select the new "Sales Office" InfoObject from the InfoCube.

Figure: Selection of InfoObject "Sales Office" from the InfoCube © SAP AG

The desired result is displayed.

	A	B	C	D	E
1	Query for SCD				
2					
3	Structure				
4	Sales Office				
5	Sales person				
6	Calendar Year/Month				
7					
8	Sales Office		Sales person	Calendar Year/Month	Gross sales volume
9	1010	Hamburg	MÜLLER	01.2005	120.000,00 EUR
10				03.2005	100.000,00 EUR
11				Result	220.000,00 EUR
12			SCHMIDT	01.2005	80.000,00 EUR
13				03.2005	100.000,00 EUR
14				Result	180.000,00 EUR
15			Result		400.000,00 EUR
16	9000	Magdeburg	BAUER	01.2005	100.000,00 EUR
17				03.2005	100.000,00 EUR
18				Result	200.000,00 EUR
19			HUBER	01.2005	200.000,00 EUR
20				02.2005	100.000,00 EUR
21				Result	300.000,00 EUR
22			Result		500.000,00 EUR
23	9200	Montreux	HUBER	03.2005	300.000,00 EUR
24				Result	300.000,00 EUR
25			MAIER	02.2005	150.000,00 EUR
26				03.2005	200.000,00 EUR
27				Result	350.000,00 EUR
28			SCHULZE	01.2005	140.000,00 EUR
29				03.2005	110.000,00 EUR
30				Result	250.000,00 EUR
31			Result		900.000,00 EUR
32	Overall Result				1.800.000,00 EUR

Figure: Display of the Historical Truth © SAP AG

VI

Enterprise Planning with SAP BW BPS

Enterprise planning based on decision-support tools is increasingly becoming a critical success factor for companies. The SAP Business Information Warehouse enables enterprise planning based on the OLAP approach.

I

Planning Processes

Experience shows that the planning processes at most companies are extremely complex on one hand, yet on the other hand have to be dynamically adjustable, in order to keep up with market demands. Enterprise planning based on decision-support tools is increasingly becoming a critical success factor for companies.

While many companies are still using spreadsheet-based planning approaches, special software solutions for enterprise planning are increasingly making inroads. We differentiate here between software that is targeted at a specific business application area (such as cash flow planning, balance sheet planning, or profit & loss planning) and freely configurable software solutions.

In this context, "freely configurable" means the system is not characterized by predefined content; instead, the planning process is modeled individually in the system – which is usually based on the OLAP approach. Due to the custom nature of the planning process, such solutions have proven to be superior in practice. The SAP Business Planning and Simulation component, which is integrated in SAP BW 3.5, belongs to the group of freely configurable systems.

Business Scenario

The following extended case study will illustrate the basic functions and potential uses of SAP BW BPS.

Scenario

Due to the numerous interdependencies between the individual planning areas, management at Motorsport AG has decided to implement OLAP-based enterprise planning.

The new solution is to be integrated with the actual data from sales controlling, and needs to support extensions and enhancements flexibly. The solution scope needs to cover the entire cycle of sales, revenue, cost, and margin planning, down to the calculation of the planned results by article and sales office.

Planning Process

The starting point for planning is the country-specific sales prices for the articles. Based on this information, management develops targets for improving sales, reducing costs, and boosting margins (top down). The individual sales office managers are now responsible for conducting quantity and sales planning for their respective offices, taking regional market factors into account. In addition to differing articles, the different distribution channels also have to be considered. The detailed planning will then take the central sales and revenue targets into account. Based on this information, the controllers in the respective sales offices plan the costs and attainable margins in their regions (bottom up).

By aggregating the regional results, the planned results for Motorsport AG can be calculated automatically, and compared against the targets defined by management.

Planning Instantiation

Our case study can be defined as follows with regard to the usual planning system:

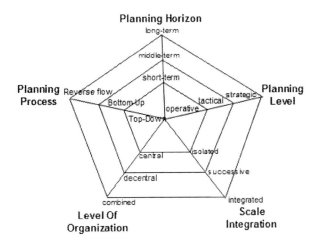

Figure: Target Instantiation of the Planning System

The solution scope needs to cover the entire cycle of sales, revenue, cost, and margin planning, down to the calculation of the planned results by article and sales office.

The starting point for planning is the country-specific sales prices for the articles. Based on this information, management develops top-down targets for improving sales, reducing costs, and boosting margins.

In the next step, the individual sales office managers are responsible for conducting quantity and sales planning for their respective offices, taking regional market factors into account. In addition to differing articles, the different distribution channels also have to be considered. The bottom up-based planning will then take the central sales and revenue targets into account.

Based on this information, the controllers in the respective sales offices plan the costs and attainable margins in their regions.

By aggregating the regional results, the planned results for Motorsport AG can be calculated automatically, and compared against the targets defined by management.

II

Planning with SAP BW BPS

The SAP BW BPS planning system works directly with the metadata (InfoObjects and InfoCubes) and master data defined in the SAP BW Administrator Workbench. The difference compared to mere data analysis is that in the planning process, planning values are written back to the InfoCube.

Transactional InfoCubes

To enable high-performance processing of frequent updates to (small) data volumes, the InfoCube where the planning process is carried out is classified as transactional.

The planning cube has a similar structure to the InfoCube from the sales case study, but also has the characteristics Division, Company Code, and Country in the InfoCube so planning data can be saved for these characteristics. In addition, a Version field exists to differentiate between the different data versions within planning (which can arise from different planning runs, for example).

The actual planning process is implemented as an interaction between input screens for entering planning figures manually and planning functions that process the data automatically.

Several example planning and screens and planning functions are shown below.

Planning Sales Quantities

The sales office managers use the Web interface below to plan the sales quantities. The relevant articles (street motorcycle, scooter, motocross motorcycle) are planned on a quantity basis, including discounts.

Sales Office

Save | Exit | Refresh

Selection

Year for actuals 2004

| Product yearly | Product monthly | access. yearly | access. monthly | sum |

Selektionsauswahl

Produkt Scooter 125 (1)

Quantity Wholesale	1.000,000	PC	1.026,535	PC	993,000	PC
Quantity Retail	1.010,000	PC	1.145,269	PC	1.108,000	PC
Quantity Internet	800,000	PC	1.041,918	PC	1.008,000	PC
Price per Unit Wholesale	4.973,00	CHF	4.973,00	CHF	0,00	CHF
Price per Unit Retail	5.471,00	CHF	5.471,00	CHF	0,00	CHF
Price per Unit Internet	5.272,00	CHF	5.272,00	CHF	0,00	CHF
discount Wholesale	5		10		10	
discount Retail	17		5		5	
discount Internet	13		7		7	
Revenue net value Wholesale	4.724.350,00	CHF	4.594.457,75	CHF	4.293.885,74	CHF
Revenue net value Retail	4.586.339,28	CHF	5.952.488,31	CHF	5.563.073,19	CHF
Revenue net value Internet	3.669.311,99	CHF	5.108.481,73	CHF	4.774.282,00	CHF

Figure: Planning of Annual Sales by Article and Distribution Channel in the Web
© SAP AG

In contrast, items in the accessories article group are planned in total, on a value basis.

Sales Office

| Save | Exit | Refresh |

Selection   ☐

Year for actuals 2004

| Product yearly | Product monthly | access. yearly | access. monthly | sum |

Product	Distribution Channel	Currency	📋			
Leather Jacket	Wholesale	CHF	○	100.000,00	372.513,16	348.143,14
	Retail	CHF	⊙	200.000,00	432.949,52	404.625,72
	Internet	CHF	○	200.000,00	395.733,74	369.844,62
Helmet K4 black	Wholesale	CHF	○	150.000,00	332.572,53	310.815,44
	Retail	CHF	○	170.000,00	393.028,75	367.316,57
	Internet	CHF	○	180.000,00	364.638,06	340.783,23
Inspection	Wholesale	CHF	○	150.000,00	414.898,61	387.755,71
	Retail	CHF	○	200.000,00	503.727,74	470.773,58
	Internet	CHF	○	170.000,00	446.787,96	417.558,83
Overall Result				1.520.000,00	3.656.850,07	3.417.616,84

Figure: Planning of Annual Sales by Accessory Group and Distribution Channel
© SAP AG

Applying Formulas

In general, formulas and formula extensions within SAP BW BPS not only enable calculations between key figures, but also calculations within any characteristics. In addition, the FOX (FOrmula eXtension) generator features syntax elements that it shares with procedural programming languages, such as variables, branches and loops. This makes it possible to perform any type of calculation within the OLAP cube without having to rely on ABAP programming.

In one example, the margin at a company could be calculated as follows:

Calculation

Margin in % =
    [Sales Price
    - Sales Price * Discount%
    - Interunit Transfer Price
    - Interunit Transfer Price * (OH% R&D + OH% Sales + OH% Administration)
    - DC R&D – DC Sales – Special DC Sales)
    ] / Sales Price * 100

OH%   = percentage overhead cost share
DC   = direct costs

This calculation is implemented with a planing formula.

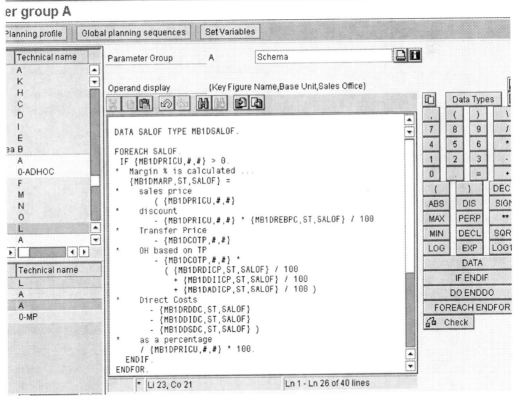

Figure: Planning Function: Calculate Margin from Type Formula © SAP AG

VII Bibliography

Codd, E.F.; Codd, S.B.; Salley, C.T. (1993): Providing OLAP (On-line Analytical Processing) to User Analysts: An IT Mandate, White Paper, Codd & Date Inc.

Fayyad, U. (1996): Data Mining and Knowledge Discovery: Making Sense Out of Data. In: IEEE Expert - Intelligent Systems & Their Application: No. 5.

Inmon, W. H. (1993a): Building the Data Warehouse. 1st Edition, New York et al.

Inmon, W. H. (1993b): Impervious to Change. In: Database Programming and Design: 3/1993, S.76-77.

Inmon, W. H. (1993c): Client/Server Anwendungen. Planung und Entwicklung, Berlin/Heidelberg/New York.

Inmon, W. H. (1994): What is a Data-Warehouse? Prism Solutions, Tech Topic, Vol. 1, No. 1, Sunnyvale.

Inmon, W. H. (1996): Building the Data Warehouse. 2nd Edition, New York et al.

Inmon, W. H.; Hackathorn, R. D. (1996): Using the Data Warehouse. Wiley, New York et al.

Kimball, R. (1996): The Data Warehouse Toolkit. Practical Techniques for Building Dimensional Data Warehouses. John Wiley & Sons, New York 1996.

Kimball, R.; Reeves, L.; Ross, M.; Thornthwaite, W. (1998): The Data Warehouse Lifecycle Toolkit – Expert Methods for Designing, Developing, and Deploying

Data Warehouses. 1st Edition., Wiley, NewYork 1998.

Kimball, R.; Ross, M. (2002): The Data Warehouse Toolkit – The complete Guide to Dimensional Modeling. 2nd edition, Wiley, New York 2002.

Pendse, N.; Creeth, R. (1999): The OLAP-Report, Business Intelligence, London, http://www.olapreport.com; 02/12/2000.

Rockart, A.; DeLong, D.W. (1988): Executive Support Systems, Homewood, Illinois.

SAP AG (2002): Data Warehousing mit mySAP Business Intelligence. White Paper, Version 1.1.

Printed in the United States
121113LV00003B/22/A